Duties and Powers

Prepared by

Beachcroft Stanleys, Solicitors

ACKNOWLEDGEMENT

The authors would like to thank Professor Tomlinson and the members of his committee for their help and comments during the preparation of this report. They would also like to thank staff at the Further Education Funding Council, the Disability Unit of the Department of Social Security, and the Department for Education and Employment.

Beachcroft Stanleys
20 Furnival Street
London EC4A 1BN
Telephone 0171 242 1011
25 March 1996

Note: *This report is not intended to provide an exhaustive statement of the law. It should not be relied upon as the basis for any decision or legal action and detailed professional advice should always be sought.*

STOP PRESS

On 27 June 1996 the Court of Appeal allowed the applicant's appeal in the case of <u>R v Gloucestershire County Council ex parte Mahfood</u>, agreeing with the analysis in this report (in chapter 1, 'Duties and Resource Constraints') that the High Court's decision in this case was wrong. An appeal to the House of Lords is currently under way.

CONTENTS

Introduction

∙∙∙∙∙∙∙∙∙∙∙∙∙∙∙∙∙∙∙∙∙∙∙∙∙∙∙∙∙∙∙∙∙∙

1.   In 1995 the Learning Difficulties and/or Disabilities Committee chaired by Professor John Tomlinson asked for a report on the law governing the provision of education and other services to students with learning difficulties and/or disabilities. In November 1995 the committee commissioned a supplementary report covering further areas. This report is a consolidation of the two earlier reports produced for the committee.

2.   The authors' intention has been that the report will be fully accessible to those without legal training. We hope that we have succeeded. At the same time the areas of law dealt with are both complex and far ranging, and to enable the committee to draw attention to any areas in which it might feel the law is defective it has been necessary both to go into some detail and to address uncertain and complex legal issues.

3.   The report both gives a general discussion of the important aspects of the law relating to public bodies and their duties, and sets out the specific duties towards students with learning difficulties and/or disabilities owed by a wide range of agencies. In response to the specification set by the committee, the areas covered are:

- the meaning of legal duties and powers;

- the difference between target and specific duties;

- the effect of a body's lack of resources on its obligation to carry out its duties;

- how duties are enforced;

- an overview of the duties and powers of each of the agencies providing students with services in the fields of:

    – education;

    – social services;

    – health (both physical and mental);

    – employment and careers;

    – social security;

    – transport;

- the various definitions of learning difficulty and disability used by the agencies, the differences between such definitions and their interpretation by the courts in practice;

- the various age dimensions to the duties and powers of the various agencies;

- guidance applying to each agency and the status and implication of such guidance and relevant charters and in particular the Charter for Further Education and the requirement that a charter should be drawn up by each further education (FE) college;

- the duties, powers and other responsibilities of agencies for collaboration with each other and discussions of any lack of interaction together with relevant opportunities and constraints;

- issues relating to transition of students beyond further education, for example, discussion of legislation that provides for adults as well as young people and effecting the training and employment of people with learning difficulties and/or disabilities.

4.   The law is stated as at 25 March 1996.

The Meaning of Legal Duties and Powers

GENERAL

Meaning

5.   The essential difference between legal duties and powers is that a legal duty is obligatory, whereas a power confers on the person to whom it is given a discretion whether or not to act and also, in many cases, in relation to what action to take.

6.   It is usually quite obvious from legislation or regulations whether Parliament intended to confer a duty or a power. For example, duties are often expressed by use of the words 'shall' or 'must' or by an express statement that a person or agency has a duty (either general or specific) to do something. Similarly, where Parliament intends to confer power it quite often expresses this by saying in an Act that an agency 'may' take a certain action. Taking an example at random, section 20(3) of the Children Act 1989 states that:

> (3)   Every local authority shall provide accommodation for any child in need within their area who has reached the age of 16 and whose welfare the authority consider is likely to be seriously prejudiced if they do not provide him with accommodation.

By contrast, section 20(5) confers a power:

> (5)   A local authority may provide accommodation for any person who has reached the age of 16 but is under 21 in any community home which takes children who have reached the age of 16 if they consider that to do so would safeguard or promote his welfare.

Powers to be exercised for the public benefit

7.   On certain occasions however this simple distinction is not always a sure guide, and there are many examples of courts finding that permissive language apparently conferring a power should in fact be construed as obligatory. Agencies should therefore take care not to be misled by what appears on the face of an Act. In particular, agencies should bear in mind that they have a general overriding duty in all circumstances to exercise the statutory powers entrusted to them as the public interest requires and so as to promote and not to frustrate the policy and objects of the relevant Act.[1]

8.   This general duty is illustrated by the (to lawyers) famous case of <u>Padfield v The Minister of Agriculture, Fisheries and Food [1968] AC 997</u>. The case concerned whether the Minister of Agriculture was obliged by the wording of an Act to refer a complaint that he had received to a committee of investigation or whether he was justified in his refusal to do so. The statute in question provided for a referral to take place 'if the Minister in any case so directs'. Finding against the Minister, the court held that the Minister's reasons for so refusing were inconsistent with the policy of the Act which was that relevant and substantial complaints should go to the committee of investigation in the absence of good reason to the contrary. The permissive words gave the Minister a discretion, but he was not entitled to use this discretion in such a way as to thwart the policy of the Act and was obliged in any

event to exercise his discretion to promote Parliament's intention, which was to be adjudged from taking the Act as a whole.

9. The practical effect of the above is that in order to decide whether a power must be exercised because to do so would promote the general policy of the Act, an agency needs to consider the whole statutory context in which the power is given. This will include any relevant restrictions imposed by an Act or the use of the resources of an agency.[2]

Implied powers

10. Another point to note is that agencies may have implied powers to do certain things. The courts long ago established[3] that where an express statutory power is given by an Act it will also carry with it implied powers to do any such things as are reasonably ancillary to the exercise of an express power, for example, a power to provide laundry facilities will entail an implied power to employ staff or contract with others for this purpose (unless the Act states to the contrary).

Enforcement of public duties

11. The normal means of enforcing the performance of public duties by public authorities in the courts is by the ancient remedy of *mandamus*. The essence of *mandamus* is that where an authority is shown to be in breach of its statutory duties, the court orders that authority to perform its public legal duty. However, as a remedy, *mandamus* is discretionary and the court may well withhold it where the statute under which the duty is made provides a right of appeal or other remedy for the complaining party. In practice, however, the courts have more recently grown accustomed to awarding *mandamus* freely, even when some other remedy exists.

12. There are in some cases alternatives to *mandamus*. For example, under section 57(3) of the Further and Higher Education

Act 1992 the Secretary of State can make orders to force a further education funding council or an institution within the further education sector to carry out its statutory duties.

Contractual duties

13. Aside from their duties arising under statute, it should be remembered that agencies may also have duties under contract. Contractual duties are enforceable as matters of private law and ordinary contractual remedies, such as damages, injunctions, specific performance and declaration are generally available from the courts. Contractual duties are not enforceable by *mandamus* which is confined to public duties.

14. These questions of enforcement of a body's duties are considered further at paragraph 56 *et seq*.

TARGET DUTIES

15. Although all duties require the body subject to them to take some action, what a public body is required to do in order to have discharged a duty will depend on the duty itself. In particular, it is important to distinguish between target duties and specific duties. (Whereas 'target duty' is a term coined by the courts, 'specific duty' is the authors' term used for the purposes of this report to describe any duty which is not a target duty.)

16. A typical target duty would be an LEA's duty under section 8 of the Education Act 1944, which provides that it is the duty of every LEA to secure that there are available for their areas sufficient schools for providing education for children of compulsory school age. The LEA is under a duty to see that the schools are sufficient in number, character and equipment to offer the variety of instruction and training as may be desirable in view of the pupils' different ages, abilities and aptitudes.

17. In the case of R v ILEA exp. Ali [1990] ALR 822 DC the applicant alleged that in his area there were some 400–500 children without school places, and that ILEA were therefore in breach of this duty. The court said that this was not so:

> In order to arrive at the correct interpretation of section 8 it is important to recognise that the duty which it places on the LEA is in very broad and general terms . . . it is a type of duty which is a common feature of legislation which is designed to benefit the community. . . . This type of duty can be described as a 'target duty'. . . . [T]here is built into section 8 a 'degree of elasticity'. While there are a number of standards which are required to be achieved by the LEA, the setting of those standards is, in the first instance, for the LEA alone to determine as long as those standards are not outside the tolerance provided by the section.

(per Woolf LJ)

18. The court explained the consequences of a body being in breach of a target duty rather than a specific duty. Where an LEA failed to meet the standards set in section 8, that did not necessarily mean that they were in breach of their section 8 duty. The question was whether they had taken all the steps which the statute requires to remedy the situation (ie, the apparent breach) which existed. If they had done so then despite not providing a 'sufficient' number of schools there would be no breach of duty, and as a result no-one could bring an action against the authority. Woolf LJ remarked:

> An LEA which is faced with a situation where, without any fault on its part, it has not complied with the standard which the section sets for a limited period is not automatically in breach of the section. Here I refer to changing situations which could not be anticipated, not questions of resources or priorities.

19. Thus there are two main features of a target duty. The body under the duty will have a fairly wide degree of discretion as to which outcome, of a possible range of outcomes, will be enough to have discharged the duty, and also even in a case where a body is clearly failing to provide a level of service sufficient to discharge the duty, it will not be in breach of that duty if it is not at fault and if it has taken all the steps required to remedy the situation.

20. A specific duty, on the other hand, requires a body to achieve a certain outcome. It has no, or very limited, discretion as to what is or is not a satisfactory outcome. The duty set out above at paragraph 6 from section 20(3) of the Children Act 1989 is a specific duty. Presented with a child in need, within their area, who has reached the age of 16 and whose welfare the authority considers is likely to be seriously prejudiced if they do not provide the child with accommodation, a local authority must provide the child with accommodation. Either such a child is provided with accommodation or he or she is not. There is no equivalent of the scope for discretion which wording such as 'sufficient provision' allows.

21. It is also much more likely in the case of a specific duty that any failure to achieve the required outcome, however unavoidable, will be held to be a breach of duty allowing an aggrieved party to bring an action in the courts. This is, however, a difficult question discussed further below.

DUTIES AND RESOURCE CONSTRAINTS

Introduction

22. Educational bodies and others working with students with learning difficulties and/or disabilities have to provide a range of services from a finite budget. When can such a body decline to provide a particular service because of resource constraints?

23. Three different situations must be distinguished. In some cases, the body may be under an absolute duty to provide the service for students who demonstrate particular needs. An example is the duty of an LEA to provide free transport under section 55 of the Education Act 1944 where they consider it necessary for the purpose of facilitating the attendance of people receiving certain types of education. If the LEA considers such provision necessary, then on the face of the Act they have no choice but to provide it. This is a specific duty, as discussed above.

24. In other cases, the body may only be under a duty to make 'adequate' or 'sufficient' provision to meet demand for a particular service. An example is the FEFC's duty under section 2(1) of the Further and Higher Education Act 1992 (the 1992 Act) to secure the provision of sufficient facilities for education to which that subsection applies. Because in this example the FEFC can decide (within bounds) what level of provision is sufficient, this type of duty gives a body greater discretion than the more absolute duty set out above. This is a target duty.

25. Finally, a body may have a power to provide a particular service, but no duty to do so. An example is the power (in section 2(4) of the 1992 Act) of the FEFC to secure provision of facilities for the education referred to in section 2(1) of that Act for people in respect of whom the FEFC is not under a duty to secure education.

Specific duties

26. In this case, typically, the statute creating the duty will state that if certain conditions are fulfilled (conditions which will rarely if ever have anything to do with the availability of resources), then the body must carry out some duty. It would appear from the face of such a statute that the availability of resources cannot be a reason for refusing to carry out the duty. It is possible to imagine cases in which the body simply does not have the resources to discharge its duty to all the people who meet the statutory conditions giving rise to that duty. In such a case it would seem that the body cannot avoid breaking the law whatever it does, either by spending money which it does not have or by failing to carry out a duty imposed on it by Parliament. In the case of R v Gloucestershire County Council ex parte Mahfood *The Times* 21 June 1995 the divisional court considered just such a situation.

27. This was a case concerning the provision of assistance for the frail and elderly. The relevant statutory provisions obliged a local authority, once it had identified that such a person needed assistance (for example home help), to provide whatever assistance was needed. There was no provision for the authority to consider resource availability when deciding whether or not to meet the need, so this was an absolute duty. The respondent authority had withdrawn the applicant's assistance because it could no longer afford to provide it. The applicant argued that this was unlawful.

28. The court said that this was not necessarily so. The court agreed that once a need of the type described in the statute had been identified, the local authority had no choice but to meet that need regardless of any consideration of the availability of resources. However, when the authority was performing the prior step of deciding whether or not an individual had a need

which triggered the authority's duty, one of the factors it could consider was the availability of resources.

29. In effect the court ruled that when deciding how severe a need a person must show before the assistance was 'needed' and the authority's duty arose, the authority could set the required threshold level of severity with regard to its limited resources. If the authority had a lot of money to spend on this type of service then a lot of people would be said to 'need' assistance, whereas if money was scarce then fewer people would 'need' assistance.

30. The court based this conclusion on the argument that when assessing the need of an applicant for a service, a body would inevitably compare the extent of the need of one person with another so as to arrive at a view as to who needed help more. The court said that this comparative exercise was obviously related to resources. This being so the court ruled that a body could take into account the availability of resources when assessing needs and when deciding whether it is necessary, in the authority's view, to make arrangements to meet those needs, even where the body in question is under an apparently unqualified duty to meet the needs which it assesses a person as having. The court did point out that in some cases no reasonable body could conclude that a person did not have needs which needed to be met, and in those circumstances a lack of resources could not justify the failure to provide a service.

31. Returning to the specific example in the education field given above, as a result of the Gloucestershire case it is now the law that when a local education authority is considering whether it is necessary to provide transport for any particular student it may consider the expense involved in providing that transport, and more particularly whether those resources would be better spent providing transport for some other student. However, once an authority

has decided that it is necessary to provide the transport then it must do so regardless of resource considerations. Where it could not reasonably be concluded that a student did not need transport provided then regardless of the availability of resources the LEA is under an absolute duty to provide that transport. The same reasoning applies to any other absolute duty where a body has to be satisfied that certain preconditions exist before the duty arises. Thus, for example, a student has learning difficulties if he or she has 'significantly greater' difficulty learning than the majority of persons of his age. On the Gloucestershire reasoning, whether or not a person had significantly greater difficulty in learning would depend on whether the agency responsible for him had sufficient resources to provide additional assistance. This appears to be an exact inversion of what the position ought to be.

The right result

32. Clearly the court in the Gloucestershire case was presented with a very difficult dilemma. Whilst it may very well be that the case reaches the right result, the reasoning adopted to achieve that result, and the law as stated in the case, is in the authors' view wrong.

33. In particular, in basing a large part of their reasoning on the fact that when assessing need an authority will compare the needs of one person with another, the judges appear to have accepted what they then go on to prove, which is that as resources are limited only those in the greatest need can be offered assistance. If resources were not a relevant consideration then a body would not compare one person's needs with another, but would compare each person against some objective level of need set without regard to the demands on a body's resources.

34. Likewise it is far from obvious that when an authority is considering a precedent fact to the creation of a duty such as the degree of need for transport which a student

has (a fact which turns only on such matters as the distance from home to school, the degree of disability and/or self-sufficiency of the student, and so on) it can decide whether or not a student is in need by reference to its ability to meet that need. The authors submit that the applicants in the Gloucestershire case were right to argue that a need is a need whether it can be met or not.

35. The implications of this decision are yet to be worked out. In particular, it is entirely unclear how a body's decisions on what it can and cannot fund are to be policed by the courts. Will it be enough that the body's decision is not Wednesbury unreasonable[4] (in which case bodies have an excessively wide scope for evading performance of their duties), or will the court itself decide whether or not the body has correctly judged the level of resources which should be devoted to a particular problem (in which case the courts may overstep the traditional boundary between the judiciary and the executive). Either path is fraught with danger.

36. Where a body has a power or a duty which only arises if a particular fact is true (a 'precedent fact') then the body's decision on the existence of that fact is never conclusive. The court can always form its own view on the true state of affairs, as otherwise the body would be able to decide the scope of its own powers. Thus, a rent tribunal may have the power to reduce the rent of a dwelling house. The question of whether or not a building is a dwelling house is one on which the tribunal's view cannot be final.

37. On the other hand, a body's decisions as to facts which do not affect the existence of its powers can only be interfered with by the courts on limited grounds. For example, a rent tribunal's decision on whether or not the rent of a dwelling house is reasonable could only be challenged if it was reached in bad faith, or without considering all of the relevant factors, or if it was 'outrageous' in its defiance of logic or accepted moral

standards. This is because it is inherent in the idea of giving a body a discretion that it must be free to make up its own mind on matters within that discretion, even if in so doing it reaches a conclusion with which other parties may not agree or which they even consider to be mistaken.

38. The authors' view is that decisions on, for example, whether or not transport is 'necessary' fall within the second category, even though the existence of a necessity could be argued to be as much of a precedent fact to the creation of a duty as the status of a building as a dwelling house. This is because the judgement of what is or is not necessary is of its nature subjective and discretionary in a way which the judgement of what is or is not a dwelling house is not. This being so, it is clear that the discretion to reach a final view on what is a necessity must be the body's rather than the court's. This conclusion underpins the Gloucestershire judgement, the whole point of which is, of course, that in exercising this discretion a body is entitled to take into account factors such as resource constraints which do not obviously have a bearing on what is or is not a necessity.

39. Because the court in the Gloucestershire case ruled that the availability of resources was a factor which determined whether a person had a need or not (which as argued above is a question for the public body which can only be interfered with on limited ground by the courts), it appears that unless a body's decision on the availability of its resources (and thus on whether the body is under a duty or not) is Wednesbury unreasonable, it cannot be overturned.

40. The authors' view is that this result, coupled with the unsatisfying conclusion that a person can go from being in need to not in need and back again depending not on any change in his or her circumstances but merely on the fluctuating bank balance of the body labouring under a duty in respect of those needs, shows that the reasoning in the

Gloucestershire case is flawed and should not be followed. Resource constraints ought not to be considered as a factor which bears on whether or not a need exists. In our view the correct approach is to regard resource limitations as a collateral fact which releases a body from what would otherwise be its obligations, or, possibly better still, as a factor which would persuade a court to grant no remedy against a body which was not carrying out its duties without affecting the existence of those duties at all. This being so the existence of a sufficiently extreme lack of resources to trigger this release is a question of fact on which the court would be entitled to reach its own conclusion. Any other conclusion makes the public body the ultimate arbiter of when it is under a duty or not, which, particularly in the context of these absolute duties, cannot have been Parliament's intention. This also avoids the peculiarity of a person's needs being dependent on a body's finances.

41. We are strengthened in this view by a number of cases. In R v Secretary of State for the Environment exp. Lee (1985) 54 P+CR 311, the court said:

> *The remedies in public law are discretionary remedies and would not normally be granted if an authority is doing all that it can to meet an unqualified statutory obligation.*

In our view this principle alone is enough to dispose of the problem which confronted the court in the Gloucestershire case, and to do so without watering down the obligation on an authority to carry out its duties.

42. In addition, there is authority for the proposition that a body will not be in breach of a duty if it is in fact impossible for it to fulfil that duty. So in Bradbury and others v Enfield London Borough Council [1967] 1 WLR 1331 Diplock LJ said:

> *The duty imposed upon the LEA by subsection (2) of section 10 [of the Education Act 1944, which provides*

> *that an LEA must ensure that school premises conform to prescribed standards] is one which may take some time to perform in the case of existing schools and it is not unlawful to continue to maintain a school pending the taking of reasonable and timeous steps to fulfil the requirements of the Regulations.*

(authors' addition in square brackets)

43. Clearly premises cannot be made to conform to new standards instantly, but there is no breach of duty as a result. An even stronger case is R v Northamptonshire County Council and the Secretary of State for Education exp. K [1994] ELR 397 CA. The respondent council had a duty under the Education Acts to close a failing and inefficient school once the Secretary of State had approved closure. The school was the only single sex boy's school in the area, which was served by, *inter alia*, a single sex girl's school. Providing single sex education only for girls is a clear breach of the council's duty not to discriminate on grounds of sex under section 23 of the Sex Discrimination Act 1975. It appeared that whatever it did the council would act illegally. The court said not. No court, it held, would place a public body in such an impossible situation as to have to reconcile two irreconcilable obligations. The court held that fulfilling the duty to close a failing school could not put an authority in breach of any other duty, although if it allowed discrimination to continue when that was not necessary that could constitute a breach of duty.

44. The authors submit that this is the correct approach to the problems of resource constraints and breaches of duties. Where there is no money to pay for a particular duty to be discharged, and no way of making money available, then regardless of the wording of the statute imposing the duty, a body is not in breach of that duty if it fails to provide the required service. The duty remains, but it is not breached (and the body

Duties and Powers

is under a duty to take whatever steps are possible to see that it does not continue failing to perform its duties), whereas in the Gloucestershire approach the duty itself disappears (and it is unclear whether there would be any duty to try to resurrect it). As a decision of the Court of Appeal, the Northamptonshire judgement should be preferred to the Gloucestershire judgement, which is only a decision of the Divisional Court.

45. This is clearly a point of the greatest interest to public bodies, and one on which the law is at present in an unsatisfactory state. It is to be expected that in due course a case will be taken to the Court of Appeal or the House of Lords for a definitive consideration of the law in this area.

46. It should be noted that, in the authors' view, the reasoning in the Gloucestershire case could not be extended to any absolute duty which arose merely on the proof of the existence of objective facts (rather than 'subjective' facts such as a 'necessity' for a particular service). The Gloucestershire case rules that a body can have regard to resources when considering whether there is a necessity, as result of which, as is stated above, appears to the authors to stretch the meaning of what factors can constitute a necessity almost to breaking point. Where a duty arises merely on the proof of objective facts it would be an absurdity to argue that those facts were or were not true depending on the resources available to the body under the duty. This is an additional reason for preferring the view that lack of resources operates to relieve a body of its obligations rather than that it prevents those obligations arising at all, because the Northamptonshire reasoning does not have this limitation.

Target duty

47. If it is legal for a body to fail to fulfil an absolute duty which it would otherwise have to fulfil because it has no resources to pay for the cost of the services needed, then where the body is merely under a target duty, it cannot be any less lawful to take resources into account and to fail to discharge the duty where resources are not available.

48. However, correctly understood, it appears that it cannot be any more lawful for resources to play a part in a failure to fulfil a target duty than was the case when considering an absolute duty. The essential difference between a target duty and an absolute duty is that in the first case the public body has a discretion of its own as to what constitutes an 'adequate' or 'sufficient' level of provision, whereas in the second case the body has no choice but to provide the specified service.

49. However, the resources available to pay for provision seem no more relevant to the question of whether a particular level of provision is adequate than they do to the question of whether a particular level of need triggers the performance of an absolute duty. The authors submit that resource constraints should be regarded as a fact which, if established, will excuse a body which is providing an inadequate or insufficient level of service, rather than a factor which, somewhat implausibly, can turn the previously inadequate into the adequate.

50. It is worth noting however that in some cases a due regard to the need to conserve resources can be a factor to consider when deciding whether a target duty has been met or not. For example, sections 2 and 3 of the Further and Higher Education Act 1992 provide that when discharging its function to secure the provision of sufficient or adequate facilities for certain types of education, a further education funding council shall make the most effective use of the council's resources. The steps the councils take to discharge their duties will therefore be governed at least in part by the need to make the most effective use of resources.

Powers

51. Where a body merely has a power to provide a service, it is clearly for that body to decide, having considered all of the relevant factors, whether or not to make that service available to the student. When considering the exercise of this discretion the body must recall that it has been given a discretion only to further the objects of the enabling Act or statutory instrument, and the discretion must be exercised in that light. Likewise a discretion must be exercised, and a body is not allowed to adopt a rigid policy which fails to consider the facts of each case.

52. It is possible for a body to take availability of resources into account when considering whether or not to provide a discretionary service in a way which is not possible when the body is considering the discharge of its duties.

53. When considering the exercise of a discretion a body must consider all of the relevant factors bearing on its decision. Clearly the cost of providing a service is a relevant factor to consider when deciding whether or not to make the service available. This is particularly so when the expense of providing one service is weighted against the impact that that expense might have on other services. A body responsible for administering public funds is generally under a duty to see that they are properly administered (see for example Bromley London Borough Council v Greater London Council [1983] 1 AC 768). Part of this duty is seeing that the body achieves value for money in its spending, which is to say that the body achieves the maximum benefit from its use of resources. Thus bodies are under a duty to balance the cost of each discretionary service, and the benefit to the community of providing it, and to apply their resources in the way which seems to them to achieve the maximum benefit.

54. However, a warning note must be sounded. As stated above, a discretion is given to be exercised, and whilst a body may lawfully have a general policy which it applies in the 'run of the mill' case the body must not 'shut its ears to an application' merely because the general policy indicates that it should be rejected. There must always be a genuine exercise of a discretion. An applicant must always be allowed to argue why his case should be granted notwithstanding a policy to the contrary, and a body must always listen to those arguments and give them genuine consideration

55. Thus a body which decided that, as it had no resources available, it would never exercise a discretion in an applicant's favour no matter how extraordinarily deserving that applicant's case was, would be acting unlawfully. In R v Warwickshire County Council exp. Collymore [1995] ELR 217, in a climate of severe strain on resources, the respondent council adopted a policy of rejecting all applicants for a discretionary award for a grant under section 2 of the Education Act 1962. However, rejected applicants were given a right of appeal so that they could argue that their case should be treated as an exception. The council warned them that to succeed they would have to show the most exceptional circumstances. The court said that in principle this was lawful. However, in fact, during the three years that the policy had been in operation the council had received approximately 300 appeals and had rejected them all. The court had no difficulty in deciding that this showed that the policy was being implemented far too rigidly and that as a result it was unlawful. Therefore, however restricted a body's resources may be, it cannot for that reason adopt a rigid policy that it will never exercise one of its discretionary powers.

REDRESS AND REMEDIES

Introduction

56. It is almost inevitable that students or their parents will not always agree with the level of provision which has been made for the student. Where this is the case the student may seek redress against the body which he or she feels is not providing sufficient support.

57. The avenues open to the student in this position depend greatly on the exact nature of the complaint which is being made, on the body which it is alleged is doing less than it should, and on the source of the duty which it is alleged that the body is not performing. For this reason this report can only outline the options open to the student. In particular, it is not feasible either in practice or in principle to set out all of the actions which a student might take to enforce each one of the duties which might be owed to him or her. This is because a decision on what might be an appropriate form of action to seek redress (or whether redress is available at all) can depend not only on what duty it is alleged has not been fulfilled but also on the exact facts of the case. Thus any generalisation could be dangerously misleading. These paragraphs instead set out the four main means of redress applicable in this context and consider when each is likely to be available and the particular features of each type of action.

58. A student's four options are a) an appeal to a specialist tribunal or committee, b) an action for breach of contract, c) an action in tort, and d) an application for judicial review (ie, a public law action).

Specialist tribunals and other 'informal' procedures

59. In referring to an appeal to a specialist tribunal it is intended to encompass a wide range of possible procedures and the term 'tribunal' is intended to include all of these.

60. There may be a tribunal set up by statute. The Special Educational Needs Tribunal is the prime example. A right to appeal to this tribunal, in a case over which it has jurisdiction, is enshrined in the Education Act 1993. The procedure which will be followed by the tribunal, and its powers, are set out in some detail in the 1993 Act and in regulations made under it (the Special Educational Needs Tribunal Regulations 1995 S.I. 1995/3113). Alternatively, there may be a right of appeal to the Secretary of State.

61. Alternatively, a body may be obliged by statute to reconsider its decision if requested to do so, or to keep its decision under review so that a parent or student can draw any changed circumstances to its attention. This too creates a *de facto* right of appeal or rehearing.

62. Less formally still, a body may offer a right of appeal in the discharge of a statutory duty, without being obliged to do so. An example would be the FEFC, which is under a duty to have regard to the needs of people who have learning difficulties, and as part of the machinery it has put in place to ensure that it discharges that duty offers an appeal procedure from any assessment of need which it makes. This decision to offer an appeal was one taken by the FEFC itself, and it could not have been criticised if it had decided to discharge its duties in some other way.

63. A student should not overlook any grievance procedures offered by a college. Colleges are obliged by the Charter for Further Education to have machinery whereby students can raise complaints on course content, the provision of facilities, and so on, and the fact that such procedures are internal and probably without legal underpinning does not mean that they cannot be an effective avenue of redress.

64. A final type of tribunal which may be relevant is an institution's visitor (if any). The visitorial jurisdiction is not considered at

length in this report, as it is likely only rarely to be of relevance. (Only chartered universities have visitors.) Essentially, the visitor is appointed as the final judge of anything relating to the regulation of the university's internal affairs, and the grounds on which even the courts can interfere with a ruling of the visitor are limited. Interesting though this jurisdiction is, it is not considered further here.

65. Although these five types of tribunal are different in many ways, they share certain common features. The first is that as an avenue of redress, a student can clearly only bring his or her complaint to a specialist tribunal if one exists which has jurisdiction to hear his complaint. In many cases this will not be so and if the student cannot settle the dispute with the providing body informally then his or her only option will be to bring an action in the courts.

66. The most important feature of an appeal to the types of tribunal listed above is that the tribunal will generally have power to take an entirely new decision on the subject matter. This gives a tribunal a wider range of options to do justice between the two parties than a court has, as the circumstances in which a court can order a party to make some particular provision available are limited. A specialist tribunal will probably have expert knowledge or experience in the field of students with learning difficulties or disabilities which will assist it in reaching an informed and fair decision. In addition, there may be matters (principally matters involving questions of academic judgement) on which the courts will almost certainly decline to take a view. If the student is complaining about such a matter (for example, whether sufficient account was taken of his dyslexia when considering his exam performance) then his only option will be to pursue an internal appeal. Likewise, where an institution has a visitor the courts will not intervene in any matters within his or her jurisdiction at least

until the visitor has given a ruling (see Joseph v Board of Examiners of the Council of Legal Education [1994] ELR 407).

67. It is also true that an appeal to a tribunal ought to be quicker, cheaper and easier than bringing an action in court. It is unavoidable that once both sides to a dispute have instructed lawyers and issued or defended proceedings, attitudes harden, and the scope for a compromise of the dispute is reduced. Pursuing an informal remedy may avoid this. In this context it may be regrettable that the Special Educational Needs Tribunal has been set up with a considerable number of detailed rules governing its procedure and powers. It is to be hoped that this tribunal does not develop as have the industrial tribunals, which were also intended to be an informal forum for use by members of the public without the assistance of lawyers, but in which each party really requires professional assistance if their case is to be properly conducted.

68. Finally, if a student wishes to bring an application for judicial review of a body's decision, a court will usually require the student to have exhausted all other possible means of redress. Thus an attempt to make use of an appeals procedure, if one is provided, will usually be a precondition to an application for judicial review.

69. Before considering the types of legal action a student may take, one detailed point should be disposed of. Where a student has appealed to the Special Educational Needs Tribunal then if he or she is still dissatisfied with his or her treatment, the next step is an appeal to the High Court under Order 55 of the Rules of the Supreme Court. The Court of Appeal made it clear in the case of R v Special Educational Needs Tribunal exp. South Glamorgan County Council *The Times* 12 December 1995 that this is the procedure which must be followed, and that the student cannot apply for judicial review instead. The reason for this is a point of tribunal law

which would not apply to the other types of tribunal discussed above and need not be considered here.

Actions for breach of contract

70.   Obviously for a student to be able to claim that a breach of a duty owed to him or her is a breach of contract there must be a contract in existence. A contract is merely a set of promises made as a bargain by each party intended to be legally enforceable. Even where a body promises a student that it will carry out its statutory duties towards him or her, that does not create a contract. Whilst it is not wholly inconceivable that some other body or individual might form a contract with a student, it is almost certainly the case that the only body with whom a student could successfully allege that a contract had been made would be the college that he or she attended and the rest of this section refers only to colleges for this reason.

71.   The authors' view (with which the DfEE do not necessarily agree) is firmly that the relationship between a student and his or her FE college is primarily contractual. It is beyond doubt, as the DfEE freely agree, that a student attending a higher education (HE) institution has a contract with the institution. It is also clear in our view that a prospective student who has been offered a place, and has accepted, has a contract with the college (see Moran v University of Salford [1994] ELR 187). In certain cases (again, the chartered universities) a student may also be a member of the institution, but this is not a possibility which affects this discussion.

72.   It is noted elsewhere that there are very few statutory duties imposed on colleges in relation to students with learning difficulties or disabilities. For these reasons a student dissatisfied with the provision made by a college will probably look to an action for breach of contract for redress, although there is no reason why a college should not be subject to judicial review in an appropriate case.

73.   If the student alleges a breach of contract, the issue between the college and the student will probably be a simple one — what has the college promised to do for the student, and has it kept that promise? The answer will depend on the facts of each case. As discussed below, colleges should be aware that statements in a prospectus (for example, that a building is suitable for use by disabled people or that extra help is available for those with learning difficulties) or in codes of conduct or statements of policy in relation to, *inter alia*, disabled people, can be implied into the contract with the student, as could statements made by college staff, if it would appear to a reasonable person that the statement was intended to amount to a contractual promise. It is possible that a disability statement made pursuant to the Disability Discrimination Act 1995 could also be implied into a contract.

74.   It is at least arguable, in the authors' view, that the offer of a course to a student, if made with full knowledge of the student's disability or learning difficulty could amount to a promise that the course is suitable for the student and/or that the student will be given the help needed to overcome his or her handicap and participate in the course. This would not be the case where the college expressly stated to the student that such help would not be available, or could not be guaranteed, as in that case it would be clear that the college was not undertaking any contractual obligations in that regard.

75.   An action for breach of contract may be begun at any time up to six years after the breach complained of, and it may be brought in either the High Court or the County Court. In either case the action will usually take over a year to bring to court, although by asking the court for interlocutory relief (ie, for some remedy to be given whilst the case is prepared for trial) the student may be granted a remedy in a more useful timescale. In the Moran case the final hearing on interlocutory relief in the Court of Appeal

was held within one month of the issue of the writ. A student who succeeds in an action for breach of contract will be entitled to compensation sufficient to put the student, so far as is possible, in the same position as he or she would have been in had the contract been performed properly. He or she may also be entitled in an appropriate case for an order from the court compelling the college to carry out its obligations under the contract.

Actions in tort

76. The essence of contract is agreement. If a party agrees to take on some obligation then the courts will enforce that undertaking. The law of tort proceeds on an entirely different footing. The law regards some obligations as so important that they are imposed regardless of any agreement. Thus the range of bodies which a student could potentially sue in tort is wider than the range of bodies which could be liable in contract. An action in tort is essentially an allegation by the student that some body has not carried out a private law obligation which is imposed by the law on that body, and that as a result the student has suffered a loss. For example, the law imposes a requirement on car drivers that they drive carefully. If a student were injured by a careless driver taking him or her to college, the student would sue the driver in tort.

77. However, just as there must be a contract before a student can sue for its breach, so there is an equivalent in tort. A student cannot sue a body in tort unless that body owed him or her a 'duty of care' in carrying out its functions. The question of when a body owes a student a duty of care, involving as it does a consideration of whether the body's obligations to the student are so important that liability should be imposed by law, is never straightforward. The courts have at various times indicated the factors which point towards or away from a duty of care being imposed, but ultimately, and despite strenuous efforts to

disguise the fact, the decision as to whether to impose a duty is one of public policy as perceived by the courts. A general discussion of when such a duty will be implied is beyond the scope of this report.

78. In recent years a number of cases have been brought against education authorities alleging that they were careless in carrying out their duties towards the plaintiff (a child with special educational needs) and that this carelessness was a breach of a duty of care owed to the child. The authorities argued that they owed no such duty. If the children were right, then they could have succeeded in an action in tort and claimed for any damage caused by the careless assessment. This would extend to damages for reduced employability, if the authority's carelessness (rather than the child's educational difficulties) had reduced the child's prospects on the job market. A sample of test cases was heard by the House of Lords in the summer of 1995. Their decision was given in X v Bedfordshire County Council [1995] 3 WLR 152, which is now the leading authority in this regard in the education field. (It should be noted that although the cases concerned schoolchildren and LEAs, the legal principles laid down are applicable generally across the education field.)

79. The House of Lords held that the authorities themselves did not owe a duty to be careful to such a child. The House of Lords applied well-known legal principles and reasoned that as the aim of the special educational needs regime was to benefit society as a whole by offering help to a disadvantaged group, rather than to create individual rights which could be enforced by an action for damages, there could be no action in tort. This indicates that a duty should not be imposed. The court concluded that although an authority was clearly under a duty to run the special educational needs apparatus carefully and properly, that was not a duty which an individual child could enforce by suing a careless authority in tort.

80. Thus the law on the liability in tort of any body which has duties in regard to disabled people or those with learning difficulties is as follows. Unless it can be argued that those duties were imposed with the primary intention of benefiting that individual, so that if the duties were not carried out there should be financial compensation, there is no liability in tort. It is not enough that the duty was imposed with the intention that society as a whole should benefit from ensuring that disadvantaged members are given assistance. In that case there will be no duty of care and no action in tort. This is a subtle distinction to say the least, and serves to illustrate the truth of the observation above that such distinctions are really made on policy grounds rather than strict legal reasoning.

81. The conclusion must be that in the light of the Bedfordshire case it is very unlikely indeed that a body owing duties to disabled people or those with learning difficulties will be liable in tort if those duties are carried out carelessly. (The principal exception will be where the body breaches one of the duties imposed by the Disability Discrimination Act 1995, if and when it is brought into force. That Act expressly states that breaches of duties imposed by it constitute discrimination and that a discriminator may be sued.)

82. However, a body such as an LEA can be liable in tort in two ways. It can be liable for its own torts, and also liable for the torts of its employees committed during the course of their employment (known as vicarious liability). The House of Lords ruled out an authority being 'personally' liable. But, it went on to say, there was no reason why an authority (and hence any body carrying out duties) should not be vicariously liable. Thus if an authority used educational psychologists (or any other member of staff) to assess and determine a child's needs then the authority could be vicariously liable to the child for the psychologists' carelessness.

Importantly, the House of Lords said that this extended to the carelessness of a headmaster of a school. The authors' view is that this vicarious liability extends to the carelessness of any employee of a body involved in the care of disabled people or those with learning difficulties.

83. There are two components which build up to create a body's vicarious liability. The first is that the employee must be personally liable to the student. This means that the employee must personally owe a duty of care to the student, and must have been careless in carrying out that duty. The second is that carelessness must have occurred during the course of the employee's employment.

84. A detailed consideration of which employees would be held personally to owe a duty to a student is beyond the scope of this report. Factors pointing towards such responsibility would be whether it was foreseeable that if the employee was careless the student would be caused harm, and a proximate relationship with the student, which means factors such as a personal involvement with the student or an assumption of responsibility towards the student. Possession of professional skills or assumption of professional duties will also be relevant. It is to be expected that this is an issue which will be explored by the courts in the years ahead.

85. Carelessness occurring during the course of employment means that the employee must have been doing what he or she was employed to do, albeit in a careless or even a forbidden way, rather than doing something which he or she had no business to do at all. Thus an educational psychologist employed to assess children may create vicarious liability if he does so carelessly, whereas if the same psychologist offered careless advice on, for example, benefit entitlement that would fall outside the scope of the job altogether and would not create vicarious liability.

86. This vicarious liability for the actions of employees would only be excluded if it could be shown that holding the authority liable would conflict with its being able to discharge its statutory duties to the child, a point which the House of Lords in the Bedfordshire case said was not obvious.

87. Thus the position is that a body will very probably not be liable in tort itself if it carries out its functions carelessly, but it will be liable for the carelessness of any of its employees who owe a duty to the student.

88. Tort actions are brought in the High Court or the County Court and must generally be commenced within six years of the harm which the breach of duty caused. (Cases where a tort caused personal injury are an exception, as these must generally be brought within three years.) The consequence of a student successfully bringing an action in tort is that the defendant must compensate the student for all the loss which was caused by the defendant's failure to fulfil its obligations. This could include lost prospects on the job market, if those were truly caused by the tort rather than by the student's pre-existing difficulties or disabilities. The defendant could also be compelled to carry out its duties in an appropriate case.

Public law actions

89. Breach of contract and tort are private law actions. In enforcing private law the courts police the relationship between one person and another. A student may wish to bring a public law action (an application for judicial review). In a public law action the courts regulate the relationship between an individual and some manifestation of the state, and see that public bodies do what they should and do not overstep their powers.

90. A student may decide to bring an action to enforce public law rights for a number of reasons. The most common reason would be that there is no breach of a private law right

which can found an action. Alternatively, there are remedies available in public law which are different from, and often better than, the remedies which the court can grant in a private law action.

91. However, whether any particular set of facts gives rise to the right to bring an action for breach of the student's public law rights is a difficult question. Public law remedies can only be sought against actions of public bodies, and an action will only succeed where the body has acted in some way contrary to law.

92. However, the courts have adopted a wide definition of what is a public body. The crucial question is not whether a body has been set up under statute, or whether it derives its powers from some 'public' source (although that is certainly an important consideration), but rather whether the body carries out some function in which there is a 'public element' and that it does not derive its authority solely from contract or consent (per Sir John Donaldson MR in R v Panel on Take-overs and Mergers exp. Datafin [1987] QB 815). Thus it is highly likely that any body which has duties towards disabled people or those with learning difficulties will, in an appropriate case, be susceptible to judicial review. We doubt that private specialist colleges can be subject to judicial review, which is another reason for supposing that a student at a college is in a contractual relationship with the college.

93. Specifically, a further education corporation is in the authors' view subject to judicial review. They were established by statutory instrument, and are subject to articles and memoranda of government which are laid down in another statutory instrument. More importantly, however, they are the major component in the provision of further education for those who want it. Rather than provide for colleges to be owned or controlled by public bodies, and for

further education to be made available to the public in that way, Parliament has provided that the corporations are to be private legal entities provided with public funds, at least in part, via an arm's-length funding council. This change in form cannot obscure the fact that there is a real public interest in the provision of further education which is only substantially met by the corporations. The necessary 'public element' would therefore appear to be present.

94.   It also appears that other institutions within the further education sector, such as the designated institutions, would probably also be subject to judicial review. In the case of Majid v London Guildhall University (1993) *The Times Higher Education Supplement* 12 November the Court of Appeal agreed that in a proper case the actions of a limited company which was running a university could be judicially reviewed. It would be misleading to generalise too far, however. The mere fact that a body provides education does not of itself create a 'public element', for example private (ie, public) schools are not subject to judicial review. It is suggested that a decisive factor is the question whether, if the body providing the education did not exist, some public agency would step in to fill the gap. In the case of private schools the answer is no, presumably as there already exist various types of state-run or funded schools which could accommodate extra pupils. In the case of a university the answer is presumably yes, possibly because the state would feel it necessary to replace lost capacity in the higher education sector. It may be that there are some institutions providing services to disabled people or those with learning difficulties which would not satisfy this test, and those institutions would have a good argument that they were outside the scope of judicial review altogether.

95.   Not every action of a public body will create a right to challenge it by judicial review. Where the matter of which the student complains relates solely to some private relationship between the student and the body (for example a breach of contract), and does not involve the wrongful discharge by that body of any rights or duties imposed on it as a public body, then there is as a rule no possibility of judicial review. Public bodies employ staff, rent buildings, pay for utilities and so on just as private companies do, and they are not subject to any more regulation in this regard merely because they are public rather than private individuals. Judicial review exists only to see that public bodies are performing their public functions properly.

96.   Typical examples of a breach of public law would be a body failing to carry out a duty which it is obliged to perform, or taking an action which it has no power to do. Public law also bites on how and why a body takes a decision. Thus if a body takes a decision which it has authority to take, but does so without a proper consideration of all of the relevant facts, or after considering irrelevant facts, or in bad faith, then that decision will be liable to be quashed. This contrasts with private law, where a person may decide to take an action for motives good, bad or even malicious without that vitiating the action at all.

97.   Likewise public bodies are only given certain powers, and can only use those powers for the purposes for which they were granted. Whereas, for example, a private landowner can use his land for any purpose at all, a public body can only hold and manage land for the purposes for which the body was created. Thus a local authority which resolved to ban stag-hunting on its land saw that decision quashed as it had been motivated by a moral objection to hunting rather than by a consideration of whether it was for the benefit of the area (which was the purpose for which the land was held).

Duties and Powers

98. An application for judicial review must be brought without delay, and in any case within three months of the decision or action complained of. Until the legality of an action is tested in the court it is as valid in law as if it had been taken entirely lawfully. Thus, unless an application for judicial review is made timeously, an illegal action will become unchallengeable and, so far as its practical effect is concerned, legal. (The exception is that a defendant in any action may always argue, if relevant to his defence, that an action or decision is against public law and a nullity, however long ago the action or decision was taken.) The action must be brought in the High Court. Remedies are always at the discretion of the court in public law actions, even if the court finds that the respondent has acted unlawfully, and can include the writs of *certiorari* (which quashes the decision challenged), prohibition (which forbids a body from acting in a particular way) and *mandamus* (which orders a body to fulfil its public duties). Damages are not available for breach of a public law right, even if the plaintiff has suffered financial loss as a result, unless a private law right of the plaintiff has also been breached at the same time.

ENDNOTES

1   In <u>R v Tithe Commissioners (1849)</u> it was said: '. . . it has been so often decided as to become an axiom that in public statutes words [which are] only directory, promissory or enabling, may have compulsory force where the thing to be done is for the public benefit'. Courts now generally prefer to make reference to the duty to promote Parliament's intentions as indicated by the overall policy of an Act. It is questionable whether this amounts to the same thing as acting to promote the public benefit.

2   For example, the duty placed on the FEFC to discharge its powers and duties under section 2 of the Further and Higher Education Act 1992 so as to make the most effective use of resources and to avoid disproportionate expenditure (see paragraphs 123 and 124) for a discussion of this provision.

3   <u>Attorney General v Great Eastern Railway Co (1880)</u>

4   A decision which is 'Wednesbury unreasonable' is one which is so unreasonable that no reasonable authority properly considering the matter could possibly have reached it. <u>See Associated Provincial Picture Houses Limited v Wednesbury Corporation [1948] 1KB 223</u>.

Duties and Powers

Education

. . . .

THE FURTHER EDUCATION FUNDING COUNCIL FOR ENGLAND

Duties towards students generally

99.   The Further Education Funding Council (FEFC or the Council) has primary responsibility for the education of students of post-compulsory school age range as a whole including students with learning difficulties and/or disabilities.[5] These responsibilities are set out in sections 2–4 of the Further and Higher Education Act 1992 (the 1992 Act) and are expressed in terms of:

- a duty to provide sufficient[6] facilities for full-time education[7] to meet the reasonable needs of any student under the age of 19 who may want such education (a target duty);

- a power[8] to provide such full-time education to students over the age of 19;

- a duty to provide adequate facilities for part-time education suitable for the requirements of persons who are aged 16 and over and full-time education suitable for persons over 19 years old where the education takes the form of one or more of a specified list of courses[9] (a target duty);

- a power[10] to provide such full-time and part-time education facilities referred to above even when the Council is not under a duty to provide them (this allows the Council to provide facilities that are for instance more than adequate).

Additional duties owed to students with learning difficulties

100. The statutory duties of the FEFC towards students with learning difficulties[11] are set out in section 4 of the 1992 Act and are expressed in the form of an obligation on the Council to 'have regard'[12] to the requirements of persons having learning difficulties in the course of carrying out the Council's more general duties to provide full-time and part-time education under sections 2 and 3.

(1)   In exercising their functions under sections 2 and 3 of this Act, each council shall (subject to the provision of those sections) do so in accordance with subsections (2) to (4) below.

(2)   Each council shall have regard to the requirements of persons having learning difficulties.

(3)   A council shall, if they are satisfied, in the case of any person among the population of their area who has a learning difficulty and is over compulsory school age but has not attained the age of twenty-five years, that:

(a)   the facilities available in institutions within the further education sector or the higher education sector are not adequate for him; and

(b)   it is in his best interests to do so;

secure provision for him at an institution outside those sectors.

Section 4(1) – (3) Further and Higher Education Act 1992

Duties and Powers

The meaning of the duty to 'have regard'

101. Legally the FEFC's duty to 'have regard' to the requirements of persons having learning difficulties is a relatively flexible one and allows the FEFC to make its own reasonable judgement as to what should be done for any individual student according to the circumstances. This is particularly so as the duty is couched in such non-specific terms, ie, making no reference to any particular code of practice or conduct[13] or any specific recommended course of action which the FEFC should have regard to. This view of the flexibility of the FEFC's obligations is supported by case law which suggests that a duty to have regard to something does not mean slavishly following it[14] and it may therefore be concluded that no particular absolute[15] standard of provision for students with learning difficulty will be required from the FEFC in all circumstances.

102. This being said, a duty to 'have regard' does imply that the FEFC cannot simply ignore the requirements of students with learning difficulties. If the FEFC chooses to do nothing or very little to give special help to such a student, it lays itself open to being challenged in the courts in judicial review. This does not mean that a court would seek to replace its own decision as to what would be done for a student for that of the FEFC but it does mean that a court will look to see that the Council has taken into account relevant considerations and not irrelevant considerations[16] in reaching its decision and has not exercised the discretion given to it in a completely unreasonable manner.[17]

Definition of learning difficulty and/or disability in the Education Acts

103. In the Education Act 1993, a 'child' is said to have special educational needs if he has a 'learning difficulty' that calls for 'special educational provision' to be made for him. A child is taken to have a 'learning difficulty'[18] if he has:

- a significantly greater difficulty in learning than the majority of children of his age; or

- a disability which either prevents or hinders him from making use of educational facilities of a kind generally provided for children of his age in schools within the area of the LEA; but not

- solely if the language or form of language spoken at home at any time is different from the one in which he will be taught at school.

104. It can be seen from a glance at section 4(6) of the 1992 Act that in exercising its powers and duties the FEFC is expected to work on a definition of 'learning difficulty' that is almost exactly the same as that used by LEAs and schools.

> (6)   Subject to subsection (7) below, for the purposes of this section a person has 'learning difficulty' if:
>
> (a)   he has a significantly greater difficulty in learning than the majority of persons of his age; or
>
> (b)   he has a disability with either prevents or hinders him from making use of facilities of a kind generally provided by institutions within the further education sector for persons of his age.
>
> (7)   A person is not to be taken as having a learning difficulty solely because the language (or form of the language) in which he is, or will be, taught is different from a language (or form of a language) which has at any time been spoken in his home.
>
> *Section 4(6) – (7) Further and Higher Education Act 1992*

105. The only effective difference in the two definitions of learning difficulty is that references to institutions in the FE sector contained in section 4(6) of the 1992 Act are changed in section 156 of the Education Act 1993 to refer to schools within the area of a local education authority. On the transition

from school to the FE sector the student should therefore be able to be confident that the same criteria for assessment of his needs will apply except insofar as the facilities against which the effect of disability or learning difficulty is judged may differ between schools and FE colleges. The consistency in definitions should also ease the administrative burden on the FEFC as it becomes responsible for students with learning difficulties transferring into the FE sector, ie, it can make full use of assessments etc, made by the LEA in respect of the transferring pupil.

106. A point of interest in discussing the differences between section 156 of the Education Act 1993 and section 4(6) of the 1992 Act is that in section 4(6), there is no equivalent express concept of 'special educational provision', simply a definition of a person with a 'learning difficulty' and a duty to have regard to the requirements of each such person in exercising the Council's duties and powers to provide full-time and part-time education.

> (4) In the Education Acts, 'special educational provision' means –
>
> (a) in relation to a child who has attained the age of two years, educational provision which is additional to, or otherwise different from, the educational provision made generally for children of his age in schools maintained by the local education authority (other than special schools) or grant-maintained schools in their area . . . .
>
> *Section 156(4) – Education Act 1993*

107. By contrast, LEAs must show that they have provided special educational provision where it is required under the 1993 Act and an express definition of such provision is given. Effectively, this definition (set out in section 156(4) of the 1993 Act) means that LEAs must be seen to be providing something extra to help a child with special educational needs, beyond what they would

ordinarily expect to provide for a child without special needs but of the same age. The 1993 Act does not make clear how far LEAs must go in making additional provision available. However, the Code of Practice does give some help and suggests that most forms of differentiated attention, teaching or facilities for children with special educational needs will fall within the definition of special educational provision given in the 1993 Act. In particular, paragraph 1:1 of the Code discusses the recommended 'five-stage model' for identifying, assessing and assisting children with special educational needs and states:

> *Thus for example, stage 1 in the Code's model is characterised by the gathering of information and increased differentiation within the child's normal classroom work. Such special attention and help constitutes special educational provision as the term is used in the Act and the Code, and can be of significant benefit to the children who need it.*

108. Presumably the absence of a direct statutory requirement on the FEFC to provide 'special educational provision' is intended to give the FEFC more freedom in how it interprets the duty to have regard to the requirements of persons with learning difficulties. However, in view of the fact that the duty to 'have regard' cannot simply mean that the needs of a student with special learning difficulty are ignored, it is submitted that there is little practical difference between the duties placed on LEAs and those placed on the FEFC.

The components of a 'learning difficulty'

109. In the light of the consistency between the definitions of 'learning difficulty' used by LEAs and by the FEFC, the question arises as to what the definitions actually mean in practice. Taking the first branch of the definition, a student may be said to have a learning difficulty if he has significantly greater difficulty in learning than the

majority of persons of his age. The term 'significantly greater' is the first key component of the definition and is clearly intended to imply that a student who is a 'bit slow' is not meant to be viewed as having a 'learning difficulty'. The Code of Practice speaks of students with a learning difficulty as having a level of attainment significantly below that of their peers and in most cases difficulty in acquiring basic literacy and numeracy skills. The Code also indicates that some 20% of the population will be construed as having special educational needs at some stage in their school career. This statistic helps to shed light on the proportion of students that Parliament intends to be 'caught' by the definition, although it clearly relates to persons who fall under both heads of the definition[19] and not just the 'significantly greater difficulty in learning' test. (Many people of course will fall under both heads of the definition.)

110. There is scarcely any relevant case law on the use of the expression 'significantly greater' in relation to either the 1992 Act or the 1993 Act or their predecessor in this respect, the Education Act 1981.[20] The only case which discusses the meaning of these terms at all is R v Hampshire Education Authority ex parte J (1985) which establishes that the 'significantly greater' test is not just one of IQ. In this case, Mr Justice Taylor said that a child with a very high IQ could still have a learning difficulty under this limb of the definition if he had dyslexia, but was able to overcome its effects and achieve to the standards of the majority of his classmates. The judge also held that the child's dyslexia hindered his making use of educational facilities under the second limb of the 'learning difficulty test'.

111. Within reason it would appear therefore that Parliament has left it to the judgement and discretion of the FEFC and LEAs as to whether in any individual case a student has significantly greater difficulty in learning

than the majority of people of his age. Provided such discretion is exercised not unreasonably and appropriate procedures are followed to assess such difficulty then the courts will be reluctant to intervene to substitute their own judgement as to a student's capabilities for that of either the Council, an LEA or a school. This may explain the lack of any important case law in this area. However, it may also be the case that this expression, together with others discussed in this report which are not properly explained by reference to relevant case law, fall into that category of expressions which judges believe simply do not need further explanation. Only time can show if this interpretation of judicial silence is a correct one.

112. In the second limb of the learning difficulty definition, a student is said to have a learning difficulty if he has a disability which either prevents or hinders him from making use of facilities of a kind generally provided by institutions within the further education sector [schools within the area of the LEA] for persons [children] of his age.

113. The term 'generally provided' is another one of those expressions which neither Parliament nor the courts have seen fit to define and as such it must be given its plain ordinary meaning, to the extent that this is apparent. This being said, the courts have been more forthcoming on what does not constitute provision that is generally provided and this may be of some help to those obliged to employ the definition on a day-to-day basis. In particular, in the case of R v Hampshire Education Authority ex parte J (1985) the court held that just because an LEA routinely provides special units in each school to deal with various disabilities such as blindness, dyslexia, etc, this will still qualify as additional provision to the educational provision made 'generally' available. The Code of Practice in discussing what constitutes special educational provision is also of some help and, in

particular, paragraph 1:1 of the Code envisages that any additional attention to, differentiated treatment of, or additional facility for pupils with special educational needs will constitute 'special educational provision', that is, provision which is additional to that which is generally available.

114. As a final point on this limb of the learning difficulty test, it may in certain circumstances be important to recall that a 'learning difficulty' is an effect of a disability and not a disability in itself. It is possible therefore for a student to be 'disabled' within the meaning of, for example, the Children Act 1989 (the 1989 Act) but not to be prevented or hindered from using educational facilities. The difference in emphasis between the two types of definition, ie, 'learning difficulty' in the Education Acts and 'disabled' in the 1989 Act indicated that Parliament intends to impose a stricter test for access to special educational provision, than for access to the more 'fundamental' social services provided under the 1989 Act and other related welfare legislation.

Administrative implications

115. In the light of the discussion of the definition of 'learning difficulty' set out above, Parliament has clearly left both the FEFC and LEAs a significant discretion to interpret the scope of their duties towards students with learning difficulties. As discussed above, the courts are reluctant to interfere with the exercise of a discretion provided the authority concerned:

- has not acted very unreasonably indeed;
- has not taken into account irrelevant factors and/or failed to take account of relevant factors;
- has not misunderstood the law, ie, the extent or nature of their powers and duties.

116. On an everyday administrative basis, the FEFC should clearly put into place objective and well-reasoned criteria for

exercising their judgement as to whether a student has learning difficulties. The checklist-style approach towards the identification of specific learning difficulties adopted by the Code of Practice may well be a model. However, whatever procedures are put into place, the FEFC should remember that it may not adhere blindly to a set of rules as this would be an unlawful fetter of its discretion. Checklists and detailed procedures for assessment must at all times assist rather than replace the exercise of the Council's discretion.

Duty of the FEFC to seek provision outside the FE sector in certain circumstances

117. The 1992 Act implicitly envisages that students with learning difficulties will be educated within the FE sector with other students.[21] However, in circumstances where the Council is satisfied that:

- the facilities available within the FE and HE sectors are not adequate[22] for the student;
- it is in his best interests[23] to do so; and
- the student is between the ages of 16 and 25;

the Council is under a duty[24] to secure provision for that student at an institution outside the further education sector.[25] Where the Council is satisfied that such provision cannot be secured unless boarding accommodation is also provided then it must also secure this for the student in question.[26]

118. Section 4(5) of the 1992 Act also contains a power (in analogous terms to the duty discussed above) for the Council to secure provision outside the FE sector where it is satisfied that adequate provision for the student in question cannot be secured within the FE or the HE sector; a power which extends to the provision of boarding accommodation. Unlike its section 4(3) duty to secure independent provision, the Council's power under this section is not circumscribed by any upper age limit[27] which means that, in theory the Council

could continue to fund private provision for a student at any age over 25 years provided that such provision represented the most effective use of the Council's resources and was proportionate to the needs of the students in question. The Council is also not required to take a view under this section whether it is in the best interests of the student to secure such accommodation.

119. It is to be noted that in exercising all of its powers and duties to provide full-time and part-time education under the 1992 Act the FEFC is under a duty to have regard to any education of the same description which is provided by institutions outside the FE or HE sector. This means that the FEFC must have a view to education which LEAs and grant-maintained schools are providing including special needs education funded by LEAs at independent schools. This restriction on the FEFC's exercise of its powers has important implications for the divisions of responsibilities between agencies towards students with learning difficulties in the 16–19 age range and this is discussed in greater depth at paragraph 200 *et seqq*.

The definition of 'best interests'

120. As discussed, the 1992 Act[28] places a duty on the FEFC to arrange provision for a student with learning difficulties and/or disabilities where, in addition to its being satisfied that facilities in the FE sector are not adequate, the Council also considers it to be in the student's 'best interests' to provide for him in this way. The 1992 Act gives no indication as to what the Council should be looking for or taking into account in reaching such a decision and neither is there any helpful case law that might shed light on the matter.

121. In the absence of a clear steer from Parliament or the courts as to what is meant by the 'best interests' of a student with learning difficulties and/or disabilities, the FEFC can only really turn to what the expression means in everyday use, which is in fact how the courts would interpret them

if the matter ever became an issue.[29] On this basis it must be supposed that in deciding whether a course of action was in a student's best interests, the FEFC should look to the alternative forms of provision available and choose what would benefit the student most. This does not mean that the FEFC would be obligated to provide the best possible education for the student; but rather the best available option commensurate with the FEFC's other duties under the 1992 Act to make the most effective use of its resources and to avoid provision that gives rise to disproportionate expenditure.[30] Again, it may be said that Parliament has left the FEFC a discretion within the scope of its overall duty to decide what is in the best interests of any one student. Provided the discretion is exercised not unreasonably and the Council does not take into account irrelevant factors (eg, political or racial bias or prejudice) the courts will be unwilling to intervene.

Age ranges

122. Insofar as the FEFC is only required to have regard to the needs of students with learning difficulties in exercising its general duties to provide full-time and part-time education under sections 2 and 3 of the 1992 Act, there is no inconsistency in the age ranges covered by section 4 (students with learning difficulties) on the one hand and sections 2 and 3 on the other. The reference in section 4(3) to students with learning difficulties and/or disabilities aged up to 25 years should also be read in the context of sections 2 and 3 and limited by those sections. This means that the FEFC's duty to provide full-time education up to the age of 19 under section 2 is not changed by section 4(3) to a duty to provide up to the age of 25. However, the effect of section 4(3) is that if the FEFC decides to exercise its power under section 2(4) of the 1992 Act to provide full-time education for persons with a learning difficulty over the age of 19, the FEFC will then have a duty to ensure that provision is

made outside the sector where the relevant conditions are satisfied but only where the student in question is aged under 25 years.

Duties in respect of expenditure

123. In exercising its duties and powers under sections 2–4 of the 1992 Act the Council is under a duty to 'make the most effective use of [its] resources and in particular to avoid provision which might give rise to disproportionate expenditure'.[31] The obligation to make the 'most' effective use of resources is clearly a strong one. In practice, it means that the Council must consider carefully each item of expenditure and analyse whether resources could be better spent elsewhere. This question becomes particularly acute when the Council has to consider whether or not it should exercise a power or a discretion, for example, the extent to which the Council ought properly to allow its duty to have regard to students with learning difficulties to dictate its use of resources.

124. One means of enforcing efficient use of Council resources is by the Council setting conditions on the funding of sector colleges. The Council has powers to do this under the 1992 Act which, unlike the Education Reform Act 1988 (dealing with grant-maintained schools) contains no pre-determined formula for funding of colleges. Provided such conditions are based only on relevant considerations and promote the objects of the Act they are unlikely to be challenged in the courts. However, if the FEFC is considering the use of funding conditions to promote provision for students with learning difficulties, the Council must in setting such conditions bear in mind that its duty is only to 'have regard' to the needs of students with learning difficulties and that its overall expenditure should not be disproportionately dominated by this group. It is the most effective use of resources for all students that is required.

Section 52 powers

125. A further statutory provision to take into account in discussing the FEFC's duties to students with learning difficulties and/or disabilities is section 52 of the 1992 Act. This section gives the Council powers to require sector colleges[32] to admit individual named students provided the student in question is aged 19 or under.

52(1) This section applies where an institution within the further education sector provides full-time education suitable to the requirement of persons over compulsory school age who have not attained the age of nineteen years.

(2) A council may by notice given to the governing body of such an institution –

(a) require them to provide for such individuals as may be specified in the notice such education falling within subsection (1) above as is appropriate to their abilities and aptitudes, or

(b) withdraw such a requirement.

(3) The governing body of such an institution shall, for any academic year in respect of which they receive financial support from a council, secure compliance with any requirement in respect of any individual who has not attained the age of nineteen years which is or has been imposed by that council under subsection (2) above and has not been withdrawn.

Section 52 Further and Higher Education Act 1992

126. The 1992 Act gives no indication as to the circumstances in which the Council might be expected to invoke its section 52 powers. However, the parliamentary debate on the meaning of the provision points strongly to the fact that the power was intended to be exercised on an exceptional basis. A specific example given in the debate of circumstances where the exercise of the power would be appropriate was 'in the case of a young person with a special educational need for whom provision could not otherwise be made'.

In practice therefore the message for the FEFC is that it should not ignore the existence of its section 52 power but consider its use carefully and exercise it sparingly (if at all).

How the Council discharges its duties

127. The obligations placed on the Council in respect of students with learning difficulties are difficult insofar as the Council is at arm's length from the students who are taught in FE colleges which are legally and practically independent in status from the Council. Nevertheless, the legal duty to comply rests with the Council. This requires at the very minimum the FEFC's putting into place:

- the formulation of clear policies as to how students with learning difficulties and/or disabilities are to be identified and provided for. This will involve collaboration with schools, LEAs, health services and social services and may involve taking steps similar to those set out in the Code of Practice on the Identification and Assessment of Special Educational Needs;[33]

- mechanisms to ensure that the Council's policies towards students with learning difficulties and/or disabilities are disseminated amongst FE colleges;

- mechanisms to monitor the quality[34] and scope of colleges' provision for those students with learning difficulties and/or disabilities. The Council will also need to take this step to form clear judgements as to when and when not provision within the FE sector is adequate[35] for any particular student with a learning difficulty and/or disability;

- mechanisms to identify students who may need independent sector provision. This requires collaboration with LEAs where such students are transferring from school to further education and is discussed below. For older students, more appropriate liaison channels will be with social services departments (SSDs) and/or appropriate NHS bodies;

- mechanisms to monitor the quality and scope of provision at independent colleges where students may be placed and funded by the FEFC. The Council will need to be fully informed about the quality and type of provision offered by such colleges to enable it to make a proper decision as to whether attendance at such a college would be in the best interests of the student.[36]

128. One way in which the above can be achieved is through the issuing of circulars by the Council and the latest FEFC circular concerning students with learning difficulties (Circular 96/01) was published on 19 January 1996 (and replaces Circular 95/07 for the 1996/7 college year). This sets out in detail the arrangements for securing provision for students with learning difficulties in the independent sector and the division of responsibilities between the FEFC and LEAs in funding such students.

129. It should be noted that FEFC circulars do not have the force of law. However, they do play a valuable role in pointing out best practice and frequently giving more 'user friendly' explanations of the law to college heads and the like who have to implement such policies on a day-to-day basis. Circulars may also be used to establish and disseminate coherent systems for receiving information about students' needs from LEAs and parents.

130. It is noteworthy that FEFC circulars on students with learning difficulties and/or disabilities although addressed to a wide range of persons including chief education officers, heads of careers services and principals of specialist colleges outside the FE sector are relatively light on the need for inter-agency co-operation. This is an important contrast to the detailed provisions relating to co-operation contained in the Code of Practice and to a lesser certain extent DES and DfEE circulars. It is questionable whether the need for co-ordinating the work and services offered by various agencies to students with learning

difficulties is any less important as the student moves from the schools sector to the responsibility of the FEFC. To the extent that a lack of detailed guidance, or the equivalent to a Code of Practice, has or could potentially cause difficulties in practice, there may be a need to fill the gap, and if necessary to give any guidance published by the FEFC legislative backing.

Disabled students and Schedule 2 of the Further and Higher Education Act 1992

131. Section 3(1) of the 1992 Act places a duty on the FEFC to secure for the population of its area adequate facilities for both full-time and part-time education which is suitable for the purposes of persons in specified age ranges[37] where such education is provided by means of courses set out in Schedule 2 to the Act. One such type of course (paragraph (j) of the Schedule) is:

> *a course to teach independent living and communication skills to persons having learning difficulties, which prepares them for entry to another course falling within paragraphs (d) to (h) [of Schedule 2]...*

132. The means by which this duty is complied with is, of course, the FEFC-funded courses designed to meet this end.

133. The criteria by which the FEFC primarily decides whether to fund paragraph (j) courses are set out in annex B to FEFC Circular 96/01 and are as follows:

- the primary course objective is progression to a course which prepares students for entry to courses listed in paragraphs (a) to (g) [of Schedule 2]; and

- the course includes college accreditation which enables the student to progress to courses (d) to (g); or

- evidence of progression to courses (d) to (g) can be provided to the Council.

134. Clearly, the wording of paragraph (j) of the Schedule reflects an intention on Parliament's part — and is wide enough — to give the FEFC a large amount of discretion as to what courses it should and should not fund under this heading. Parliament has made no attempt to prescribe the detailed content of such courses or to set finely drawn parameters on what the FEFC may fund. Almost inevitably there is room for some dispute as to what exactly the scope of the FEFC's discretion should be and whether the criteria for funding set out in Circular 96/01 properly reflect the legislative intention behind paragraph (j).

The criteria set out in Circular 96/01

135. The FEFC have introduced a two-stage test for funding. It is important to note that this test is a policy adopted by the FEFC as to how it will identify the courses which fall within Schedule 2 paragraph (j). Two key questions are whether this test is lawful, and what courses can fall within the statutory definition contained in paragraph (j).

136. An objection to the criteria is that it may not have been the intention of Parliament that the primary course objective had to be preparation for entry to a specified course. A reading of the plain language of the Act could give rise to the suggestion that any independent living and communication course which incidentally prepared students for a course listed in paragraphs (d) to (g) could be funded. This argument appears to the authors to be misguided.

137. The limitation to courses with this primary objective is in our view lawful because it is the scheme of the Education Acts that LEAs should have a duty to provide such courses (ie, independent living and communication) in circumstances where the FEFC is not obliged by section 3 of the 1992 Act to provide them. There is therefore no question that by not applying a liberal interpretation to paragraph (j) any person should be deprived of the opportunity of attending an independent living skills course of which the primary objective was not simply to prepare the student to go on to another Schedule 2 course. The only question

that arises from the interpretation is the allocation of responsibilities between LEAs and the FEFC. This point was made in Parliament in the relevant debates on this issue.

138. The fact that other public bodies have extensive duties to provide courses of this kind tends to support the conclusion that the interpretation given by the FEFC to paragraph (j) is correct. It would appear logical and proper to imply that Parliament, by expressly referring to the need for paragraph (j) courses to be preparatory to other Schedule 2 courses, must have intended that such courses should be primarily for this purpose. Almost any independent living or communication course could after all be preparatory in some sense, which would mean duplication with the duties of LEAs, an interpretation which would appear to fly in the face of section 3(5) of the 1992 Act which says that the FEFC in carrying out its duties under section 3 should have regard to education provided outside the FE and HE sectors, and section 3(4) which provides that the FEFC must discharge its functions under section 3 so as to make the most effective use of its resources.

Courses within Schedule 2(j)

139. For a course to fall within paragraph (j) of Schedule 2, a main objective of the course must be preparation for entry to a course listed in paragraphs (d) to (g) of Schedule 2. The course need not be the 'key' which unlocks the door to the new course, as a course can still prepare for entry even if other factors temporarily prevent that entry. Immediate progression after the course ends is not required.

140. Accreditation or obtaining some qualification is not a requirement for a course to fall within paragraph (j). It is possible for a course to teach students living skills and communication without certification, and for that course to prepare for entry to other courses. However, it is the provider of the

next course who decides whether or not in fact a student can progress, and if these course-providers refused to accept unaccredited students then it would be more difficult to fund courses which did not lead to accreditation, because in practice progression would not occur.

141. As for how many students must progress from one course to another before the first course can be said to prepare the students for the second, this is really a policy rather than a legal question. The fact that some students fail to progress does not mean that the course does not prepare students for entry to another course (so that the percentage need not be excessively high) and but enough students must progress for the FEFC to be able to say without fear of contradiction that the course is genuinely preparing for entry.

142. Can a course in respect of which there are no identified potential progression routes fall within paragraph (j) of Schedule 2? The authors' view is that it cannot, except that as immediate progression is not required, it is possible for a course to have progression routes which are only intermittently available (maybe a place on the next course is not available for some years) so that the fact that there are no progression routes actually available at the time of enrolment need not be the end of the matter if such routes are likely to become available.

143. Specific further courses need not necessarily be identified at the time of enrolling on the paragraph (j) course, but if the student cannot give even one example of a course to which he or she might (all being well) progress then it cannot be said that the student is being prepared for progression.

The student's ability to progress

144. In the case of paragraph (j) (and also paragraphs (c) and (d)) it is not possible to talk of the characteristics of courses without considering the characteristics of students on them as well. This is because the course

Duties and Powers

refers to preparation for entry to other courses, and this in turn depends on the characteristics of the student.

145. For example, paragraph (e) includes courses for basic literacy in English. A course either is or is not within this description regardless of who is enrolled on it. It would be possible to teach a course in basic literacy in English to people highly skilled in the use of the language, and the fact that the course is pointless for them does not affect its nature.

146. Paragraph (c) on the other hand refers to a course to prepare students for entry to higher education. Here the characteristics of the students do make a difference. If this course were taught to people who had left school at 16 without qualifications it would prepare them for progression. If, however, it were taught to students just about to start at university then it would not prepare them for progression. They are already prepared.

147. The distinction is that some courses, such as paragraph (e), do not have to achieve any particular end, whereas others, such as paragraph (j), do have to achieve a certain goal. Where a goal has to be achieved then the ability of the student to achieve that goal is relevant. (It may be that this distinction was not intended by Parliament, but it seems logically inescapable.)

148. In practice this probably requires more of students with learning difficulties than others. The unfortunate fact is that most students are simply not known to the FEFC, but students who need a course within Schedule 2 paragraph (j) usually are. Although the FEFC funds courses under Schedule 2 rather than students, if it discovered that any particular student could not achieve the aim of a course, or did not want to progress, it seems that the FEFC should not fund that student, both because it is doubtful that that course, as applied to that student, would fall within Schedule 2, and because the expenditure would be disproportionate. Maybe unluckily the FEFC is much more likely to be in this position with regard to students with learning difficulties, but the test is the same as applied to any student.

149. This does not mean that such students cannot be funded, nor that there is no duty to provide them with courses they need. It simply means that it is LEAs rather than the FEFC which must fund them.

Is progression within the course enough?

150. No amount of progression within the course can bring a course within paragraph (j) if there is no course within one of the other paragraphs of Schedule 2 to which the student can progress, but progression within the course can be evidence of capacity to progress beyond the course and thus could cause the FEFC to decide to fund a student who otherwise it might have thought would have been unable to benefit from a paragraph (j) course.

151. If there were more, or different, courses within Schedule 2 generally then it would be easier for students to make the jump from a paragraph (j) course to another course, and so more students and more courses would fall within paragraph (j). The Secretary of State has power to amend Schedule 2 by Order, and so more of these courses which could more easily be progressed to could be brought into the Schedule without difficulty.

152. However, it appears from the wording of paragraph (j) that the FEFC should have regard not only to the course but also to the would-be student's ability to benefit from it. The exact wording of the paragraph makes it clear that it is not crucial that the course should be avowedly one which is intended to prepare students for entry to further courses of the types specified, but that that should be its practical effect. It was noted above that the FEFC criterion that the course's primary objective should be such progression was an acceptable addition to the statutory provisions, but that should not be taken to mean that it would be acceptable to ignore a

requirement in the Act that the course should also in practice prepare the student for progression.

153. Paragraph (j) refers to a course which 'prepares them [persons with learning difficulties] for entry to another course . . .'. If a student's difficulties are such that in fact the course cannot prepare him or her for progression, because no progression is possible, then it appears doubtful whether that student can be funded under this paragraph. (It also appears that, insofar as the FEFC's duty is only to secure 'adequate' facilities for such education, and in light of the fact that it must make the most effective use of its resources in so doing, that unless the FEFC were in the happy position of being able to afford to fund provision of Schedule 2 courses for all who wanted them, the FEFC could decline to fund such a course for a student who could not in fact benefit from it on the grounds that this is an inefficient use of resources which could better be utilised elsewhere.)

154. It is also worthwhile stepping back from the exact wording of the Act to consider its overall scheme. The FEFC is a body, the purpose of which is to fund education. Clearly the FEFC will fund places for students who for many reasons fail to derive much if any educational benefit from their courses. Students may fall ill, or drop out from their course for any of many reasons, or simply find the course too difficult or too easy. No funding council could avoid funding such students because they cannot be identified in advance. But it appears that the FEFC cannot have been intended to fund a course for a student when it is known in advance that he or she cannot derive any educational benefit at all from it. In that case the course becomes simply the provision of medical therapy or even simply nursing care and attendance, and valuable though such provision is, it appears that it must be the responsibility of the health service or a social services department rather than an educational funding body.

Which course providers may be funded

155. Section 3 and Schedule 2 impose no restrictions on who may be funded in respect of course provision. The operative provisions in respect of who may and may not be funded are found in section 5 of the 1992 Act. This section appears to imply that funding for Schedule 2 courses may only be given to institutions within the FE and HE sectors. However, if support is given under the auspices of the powers and duties given to the FEFC under sections 4 and 5(4) of the 1992 Act, the FEFC will have much broader powers to fund bodies outside the FE and HE sectors (the FEFC's powers to fund under this section are discussed at length earlier in this report; see paragraph 99 *et seq.*).

DUTIES OF FURTHER EDUCATION INSTITUTIONS

Statute

156. Further education institutions (referred to here as 'colleges'), unlike funding councils, LEAs or local authority social services departments, are not subject to a great many statutory duties towards students with learning difficulties or disabilities.

157. Until relatively recently the only duty imposed by statute was set out in section 8 of the Chronically Sick and Disabled Persons Act 1970. This provides that anyone providing buildings for, *inter alia*, universities, institutions within the higher education sector, or institutions within the further education sector, shall, in the means of access both to and within the building and in the parking and sanitary facilities available, conform with as much of DES design note 18 ('Access for the physically disabled to educational buildings') as is relevant. This obligation is lifted where a body prescribed by the Secretary of State is satisfied that in the circumstances it is either

not practicable to make provision or reasonable that provision should not be made

158. Enforcement of this obligation is intended to be by local planning authorities, either by informing the developers of these requirements at the stage of the granting of planning permission or, at least insofar as the design of a building with the disabled in mind is a planning matter, when deciding whether or not to grant planning permission. Although still in force, the importance of this section will be greatly reduced when the sections of the Disability Discrimination Act 1995 discussed below come into force.

159. In addition, section 5 of the Disabled Persons Act 1986 requires college governing bodies to notify the relevant social services department where a student who is regarded by the LEA as disabled is about to leave full-time education.

160. Section 52 of the Further and Higher Education Act 1992 is potentially an important source of obligations for colleges. The section provides as follows:

(1)   This section applies where an institution within the further education sector provides full-time education suitable to the requirements of persons over compulsory school age who have not attained the age of nineteen years.

(2)   A council may by notice given to the governing body of such an institution –

(a)   require them to provide for such individuals as may be specified in the notice, such education falling within subsection (1) above as is appropriate to their abilities and aptitudes, or

(b)   . . .

(3)   The governing body of such an institution shall, for any academic year in respect of which they receive financial support from a council, secure compliance with any requirement in respect of any individual who has not attained the age of nineteen years which is or has been imposed by the council under subsection (2) above and has not been withdrawn.

161. This section is relatively self-explanatory. It could be used by the funding councils to secure that a college must provide education for a named student with learning difficulties or disabilities, provided that that student is under 19 years old and requires full-time education. It should be noted that there is no power to compel the provision of other, non-educational services to that student, such as assistance with access. It is likely that the reference to education appropriate to a student's abilities and aptitudes is apt to empower the councils to require a college to make special extra educational provision needed by a particular student. This apparent gap (in that it is no comfort, for example, to a student in a wheelchair, to know that a college must provide education for him if it cannot also be compelled to provide him with access to the building) will in due course be filled by provision of the Disability Discrimination Act 1995.

162. The legal rights of disabled people will be greatly affected by the Disability Discrimination Act 1995, if and when its provisions are brought into force. (At present none of the Act, with one immaterial exception, is in force. The sections discussed next at paragraphs 163 to 172 are not expected by the DfEE to come into force before 1997.) Section 19(5) of the Act reads:

(5)   Except in such circumstances as may be prescribed, this section and sections 20 and 21 do not apply to –

(a)   education which is funded, or secured, by a relevant body or provided at –

(i)   an establishment which is funded by such a body or by a minister of the Crown; or

(ii)   any other establishment which is a school as defined in section 14(5) of the Further and Higher Education Act 1992 . . .

Disability Discrimination Act 1995 Section 19(5)

Duties and Powers

163. Subsection (6) defines 'relevant body' as including amongst others any LEA in England or Wales, the Further Education Funding Council for England (FEFC), the Further Education Funding Council for Wales (FEFCW), the Higher Education Funding Council for England (HEFCE), the Higher Education Funding Council for Wales (HEFCW), and the Scottish Higher Education Funding Council (SHEFC). As a result the provision of education will almost always fall outside the scope of the Act's anti-discrimination provisions. (It is, of course, provision of education alone which fell within the scope of section 52 of the Further and Higher Education Act 1992 discussed at paragraphs 160 and 161 above.) However, it should be noted that the provision of any other service by an educational body such as a college is not excluded from the scope of the new Act.

164. Thus a college must not discriminate against a disabled person in the provision of any service other than education, for example, catering services, or accommodation, or laundry facilities. The college could, however, discriminate in the provision of education itself without breaking the law. Whether a particular service is or is not part of the education offered by a college may be a difficult question. For example, a meal at lunchtime seems to the authors to be part and parcel of the education offered by a primary school, but a lunchtime meal offered in a university refectory does not seem to be part of university education. There will be a spectrum of possibilities. Although it is not a decisive test, any service without which the student could not receive the education ought, in our view, to be considered part of the education. Regulations are expected in December on the scope of exclusions from these provisions of the Act.

165. 'Discriminate' in this context is defined by section 20(1) as follows:

> 20(1) For the purposes of section 19 a provider of services discriminates against a disabled person if –
>
> (a) for a reason which relates to the disabled person's disability, he treats him less favourably than he treats or would treat others to whom that reason does not or would not apply; and
>
> (b) he cannot show that the treatment in question is justified.
>
> *Disability Discrimination Act 1995 Section 20(1)*

166. This definition is quite different from the equivalent provisions in the Sex Discrimination Act 1975 or the Race Relations Act 1976 and it remains to be seen how much of the substantial case law which has built up around those Acts will be applied to the new Act. A significant difference is that it is possible to defend even direct discrimination if the discrimination is justified, but that unlike the two earlier anti-discrimination statutes the new Act sets out exclusively the very limited circumstances which will constitute justification.

167. In addition to not discriminating in the provision or standard of service offered to a disabled person, a college will have to discharge a number of duties imposed by section 21 of the new Act designed to lead to the elimination of certain disadvantages suffered by disabled people. For example, a college would have to take whatever steps were reasonable in the circumstances to remove, alter, or find ways to avoid any physical feature of their buildings which made it impossible or unreasonably difficult for disabled persons to make use of any service provided (other than education). If a college failed to do so and it was impossible or unreasonably difficult for a disabled person to use a service as a result then the college would have committed an unlawful act of discrimination.

168. Any person discriminated against under the new Act may bring an action in the

County Court, and may claim any remedy which the High Court could award.

169. It should be noted that the Act only protects those with disabilities, which are defined as physical or mental impairments which have a substantial and long-term adverse effect on a person's ability to carry out normal day-to-day activities. Although many students with learning difficulties will also be disabled under this definition, there will be many who are not. It remains to be seen whether emotional or behavioural difficulties could be treated as disablement, for example. The DfEE's view appears to be that all students with learning difficulties will be protected by the Act. This is a question for the courts as they come to interpret the Act, but in view of the wide range of conditions which can constitute a learning difficulty, it is far from obvious that the DfEE is correct. It would be lawful to discriminate against a student with learning difficulties who was not disabled, as such a student would not be a 'disabled person' as defined in the Act, and would thus fall outside the scope of the Act altogether.

170. Section 30 of the Disability Discrimination Act 1995 imposes a new duty on the FEFC which will have the effect of imposing a further obligation on colleges. The FEFC is now required to make it a condition of its financial support that the governing body of an institution within the further education sector publishes disability statements at such intervals as the FEFC may prescribe. The Act defines a disability statement as a statement containing information of a prescribed description about the provision of facilities for education made by the institution in respect of disabled persons. They are not contracts. It should be noted that there is no requirement to provide information on provision made for those with learning difficulties, except where a learning difficulty is also a disability within the meaning of section 1 of the Act. 'Prescribed' means prescribed by regulations. (In the higher education sector, an institution must provide information of a 'specified' description, and 'specified' means specified by the HEFCE. Why these two provisions differ is unclear.)

171. It is clear that of themselves these statements do not require a college to make any change in the provision it makes for disabled people. It is probably the case that the sole purpose of publishing a disability statement is to inform disabled prospective students of the facilities available for them at a college (in which case clearly some steps will have to be taken, either by the college or by the funding council concerned, to publish the information to the public). However, section 30(4) of the Act provides that:

> . . . each council shall make a written report to the Secretary of State on –
>
> (a) The **progress** made during the year to which the report relates in the provision of further education for disabled students in their area; and
>
> (b) their **plans for the future provision** of further education for disabled students in their area.
>
> (Authors' emphasis)
>
> *Disability Discrimination Act 1995 Section 30(4)*

172. The requirement for colleges to inform the FEFC about the provision made for disabled students at a college and the express power given to the FEFC by the Act to impose conditions relating to the provision made, or to be made, by the institution with respect to disabled persons, means that all of the machinery is in place for colleges to be obliged to increase their provision for disabled people. The FEFC could be obliged to require such increase by the Secretary of State exercising her powers under section 7 of the Further and Higher Education Act 1992. (It is right to point out that the DfEE have indicated that there is no intention to use this section in this way.) Finally, the wording of section 30(4) set out above appears to envisage (although it does not

require) an ever-improving level of provision. Without the need for any further legislative action colleges could find themselves coming under obligations to make certain types or levels of provision.

173. It should also be noted as an entirely separate point that a college may only spend funding received from an external funding body on the purposes for which the funding was provided. Thus, if the FEFC were to pay a college additional money in order for it to make provision for a particular disabled student, or to pay for particular changes to its premises to assist in the use of the buildings by disabled people, the college would be under a duty to apply the money for that purpose.

174. These duties owed to the FEFC would be enforced by the FEFC in the same way as the FEFC enforces any condition imposed on a college's funding. The FEFC would be entitled to withhold further funding, or even to require a college to repay any sums subject to the conditions imposed.

175. It is worth noting how informal this system is. It is up to the FEFC (unless directed otherwise by the Secretary of State and within the well-known limits imposed by public law on the discretion of any public body) to impose any or no conditions for the benefit of disabled people, and those conditions could vary from college to college. The FEFC will consider, at least in the first instance, whether a college has fulfilled its obligations or not, and if it decides that it has not the FEFC will decide what (if any) action to take to enforce the obligations.

Common law

176. In addition to these statutory duties, a college will owe common law duties to a disabled student. Unlike the funding councils or LEAs or local authority social services departments, a college is in a contractual relationship with its students and with prospective students who have accepted an offer of a place at the college. The terms of such a contract could well include obligations towards disabled students.

Contract

177. It will be a question of fact, differing from case to case, as to what obligations towards a student a college has undertaken. In the authors' view it is likely that express statements in a prospectus will be taken to be terms of a contract between the student and the college, unless there is a disclaimer in the prospectus. It is also quite possible that statements made at interview or before the student accepts an offer of a place at the college could become incorporated into the contract.

178. In the authors' view it is arguable that where a college offers a place on a course to a disabled student or a student with learning difficulties, in full knowledge of the student's disability or learning difficulty, the college could be taken to have made an implied promise that any support necessary for the student to derive the full benefit of the course will be provided. This argument was advanced in R v London Borough of Lambeth, exp. MBM [1995] ELR 374 in the context of a child with special educational needs attending a mainstream school. The argument failed because the relationship between a schoolchild and a maintained school was held not to be contractual. It is to be expected that the argument will in due course be tested in the courts in a case where there is a contract.

179. During the passage of the Disability Discrimination Bill through the House of Lords, Lord Henley said that:

> *Once accepted by a college, students will be entitled to expect that they will enjoy the access and support necessary to pursue their studies.*

Whereas our view is that this may be true as a matter of contract in any particular case, the authors are unclear why Lord Henley felt able to make this remark, as there is certainly nothing in the Bill he was discussing which makes it true. From a legal point of view this comment is a red herring, as it has absolutely no effect whatsoever, and it neither increases nor diminishes the rights of students with learning difficulties.

180. There would, of course, be no scope for implying a promise of necessary support if the college expressly stated otherwise at the time of offering the place on the course. If the implied promise were held to have been made, the question of what support would be necessary for the student to derive the full benefit of the course is a matter on which, if the parties cannot agree, the courts are the ultimate arbiters.

181. Once a student is enrolled on his or her course the contract with the college is concluded. The college could not cease to provide any provision for the student which it had promised without being in breach of contract. It is, however, important to analyse carefully exactly what the college has offered. It may be in a particular case that a college will be taken to have promised to provide a certain level of support, and in another case that a college will be taken to have promised to provide such support as it is able to afford. In the first case the college would not be able to reduce its provision for any reason, and in the second case the college would be able to reduce its provision if it could not afford the support necessary. Likewise a student's disabilities or learning difficulties may worsen with time, and it will be necessary to decide on the facts of each case whether the college had undertaken to provide increased support in such an eventuality.

182. Likewise a college may or may not be entitled to discontinue or alter a course without necessarily being in breach of contract. Without a term to this effect, a college will not be able to alter a course which it has promised to a student for any reason, unless the student consents to the alteration. In practice most higher education institutions reserve an express right to alter or cancel courses, although whether such a reservation can survive the effect of the Unfair Contract Terms Act 1977, and whether that Act applies in all cases, is not clear. It is clear that a college is free to determine how a course is to be taught, and that a student cannot complain even if the emphasis or style of the course is not what he expected. (See D'Mello v Loughborough College of Technology [1970] *The Times* 17 June.)

Other private law liability

183. An additional duty owed by a college to a disabled student is the duty of care owed by any occupier of a building to his 'visitors' on the premises. (A discussion of any health and safety regulations which may apply is beyond the scope of this report.) An occupier is anyone who has a certain degree of occupation or control over a building or part of a building. Colleges will be occupiers of the buildings which they use. Under the Occupiers Liability Act 1957, an occupier is bound to take such care as in all the circumstances is reasonable to see that the visitor will be reasonably safe.

184. The amount of care which a college will have to show to discharge this duty will vary according to the characteristics of the visitor. A steep flight of stairs in poor repair may be perfectly safe for an able-bodied person to use (so that the college would not be in breach of the duty owed to such a visitor) but highly dangerous for a disabled person (so that if the disabled person injured himself on the stairs the college would be liable for compensation). See for an example the case of Paris v Stepney Borough Council [1951] AC 367 HL, (a case in the tort of negligence, but of general application) in which the House of Lords held that an employer had to be more careful in respect of an employee who had only one eye than in respect of employees who were not so disabled.

Public law

185. The case of R v London Borough of Lambeth, exp. MBM [1995] ELR 374 discussed above is of further interest as the applicant argued that regardless of a contract

she had a legitimate expectation that the school would make provision for her. ('Legitimate expectation' is a public law doctrine which states that where a public body makes representations about its future conduct to a member of the public, or where it has acted in such a way that a member of the public reasonably thinks that it will continue to act in that way, then the body may not act in a way inconsistent with the public's expectations without at least giving interested parties a chance to argue why it should not frustrate those expectations. The doctrine is undergoing development at the present, and it is possible that it will be strengthened so that bodies could be required not merely to offer a hearing before changing their minds on a policy, but also to treat the interested member of the public as they had promised.)

186. In the Lambeth case the argument failed as the court held that in fact no representations had been made to the applicant and so she had no legitimate expectation. However, it is possible that in principle a college could find itself bound by representations it makes to a student which fall short of contractual promises. It is possible that statements made in a disability statement made under the Disability Discrimination Act 1995, or in internal codes of practice or conduct, as well as in a prospectus or letters to and communications with the student could all be given legal effect in this way in an appropriate case, even if they fall short of being terms of the contract between the student and the college.

187. One important distinction between the situation in the Lambeth case and the position of a college is that there will be a contract between the college and the student (although the DfEE appear to disagree), which is not the case between a schoolchild and a non-fee charging school. The courts have held on several occasions that where two parties have regulated their relationship by a contract, each deciding what promises to make, and accepting the promises of the

other, that the scope for using rules of law in an attempt to impose further duties on one of the parties which he could have, but did not, agree to accept under the contract, is greatly reduced. The authors' view is that the existence of a contract between the student and the college, unlike in the Lambeth case, should considerably restrict the scope for the operation of the doctrine of legitimate expectation in fact if not in law. It is not certain, on the facts of any particular case, that a court would agree.

188. It will have become clear that many of a college's duties towards a student will arise out of the college's own conduct. If, therefore, a college is careful always to keep a student fully and fairly informed of its intentions with regard to any special provision which the student considers necessary it will not find itself having taken on obligations which it will not be able to fulfil.

189. So far as a college's statutory obligations are concerned, the extant provisions provide at best a patchwork of protection for students with learning difficulties or disabilities which is likely to cause confusion to all concerned. It remains to be seen how the power of the funding councils to compel a college to educate a particular student (a power which applies to a limited subset of students) will 'dovetail' with the obligations relating to services other than education contained in the Disability Discrimination Act 1995, or what effect the requirement for disability statements will have on colleges.

The Charter for Further Education

190. Citizens' charters are not legally binding and indeed have no legal basis whatsoever. In effect, they are a non-binding commitment by the various agencies concerned (each of which draws up its own charter) to perform to a particular level or standard of service. As such they give rise to no legal rights or duties and 'customers' of any particular public service can only use the

standards laid down in them to exert pressure on service providers to perform. (It may be, however, that the terms of a charter could be implied into a contract between the body and a 'customer'.)

191. Bearing in mind the lack of any definite form of redress, students with learning difficulties applying to or attending further education colleges have the 'right' under the Charter for Further Education to expect the following information and standards in addition to all the other Charter commitments to ordinary students:

> Students with learning difficulties or disabilities have the right to expect the following:
>
> - information from each college on its policies and arrangements for such students including the availability of courses (including separate courses), access to buildings, additional support such as extra staff or special equipment, a point of contact at the college;
>
> - information from the FEFC on the availability of funding a place in an independent college if a suitable place is not available in a college in the further education sector;
>
> - information on social security benefits (freephone 0800 666555);
>
> - that colleges will take into account any learning difficulties or disabilities of its students.
>
> *The Charter for Further Education (DFE 1993)*

192. The Charter for Further Education (CFE) creates a general commitment to the standards that are expected from colleges in the FE sector. However, in the foreword to the CFE the former Secretary of State for Education the Rt Hon. John Patten MP makes it clear that the Government requires each individual college to draw up their own charter to address their own individual circumstances within the overall CFE framework:

. . . achieving high standards is, above all, a responsibility of colleges themselves, because they know their customers best. There are many types of customer: students of all ages, full-timers, part-timers, a wide range of employers requiring staff with particular skills, and others in the community who want to use college services. All have different needs and priorities. . . . I therefore expect colleges to develop their own detailed charter within this national framework by summer 1994, consulting their customers and setting precise targets wherever possible, to help deliver a better service in their own local circumstances. The Further Education Funding Council will, at my request, be making sure that college charters are in place and that they are challenging and develop over time. The Council will also monitor colleges' performance against the commitment in this Charter and their own. Colleges can apply for the Charter Mark for excellence in delivering public services.

193. In drawing up or revising their individual charters, colleges and, in addition, the FEFC should, in order to follow best practice, follow the 'Disability Checklist' (the Checklist)[38] prepared by the Citizens' Charter Unit in the Cabinet Office and endorsed by the Minister for the Disabled. The Checklist sets out the ways in which the special needs of persons with disabilities should be taken account of in drawing up charters and gives statistics on the number of people in Britain who have learning difficulties and/or disabilities. The Checklist is intended to be used in conjunction with the Central Office of Information 'Informability Guide' (the Guide)[39] which gives detailed information on disabled people and how to communicate effectively with them. Colleges are not legally bound to follow the advice set out in either of these two publications in drawing up or revising their charters, but again, like the charters themselves, the Checklist and Guide ought to be considered 'best practice'.

DUTIES OF LOCAL EDUCATION AUTHORITIES, SCHOOLS AND OTHER AGENCIES

Duties and powers of LEAs towards students in schools

194. Until 1 September 1994 the regime governing special educational needs provision in schools[40] was set out in the Education Act 1981 and its related regulations but the relevant operative provisions of this legislation have now been replaced by the Education Act 1993[41] (the 1993 Act), The Education (Special Educational Needs) Regulations 1994 and the Code of Practice on the Identification and Assessment of Special Educational Needs.[42]

195. Most of the legal duties created by the 1993 Act fall on LEAs. However, there are also duties placed on the governing bodies of schools (considered in paragraph 219 below), on other agencies[43] and on various individuals. LEAs' general duty towards children[44] who have learning difficulties is set out in section 165 of the 1993 Act. This states that, in respect of those children for whom an LEA is legally responsible, an LEA must identify those children:

- who have special educational needs;[45] and

- for whom the LEA needs to determine the special educational provision[46] which any learning difficulty[47] those children may have calls for.

196. LEAs' specific duties in respect of children with special educational needs comprise:

- where the LEA considers that a child has or probably has special educational needs and that it is necessary or probably necessary to determine what provision should be made for him the LEA then has a duty to carry out an assessment of that child's special educational needs;

- in the light of that assessment and any representations[48] made by the child's parents, a duty to decide whether or not it is necessary for the LEA to determine the special educational provision which the child's learning difficulty 'calls for';

- if the LEA considers that it is necessary to make special educational provision for the child, a duty to make and maintain a statement of that child's special educational needs;

- a duty to arrange that the special educational provision set out in the statement is made for the child and that any non-educational provision specified in the statement is made in such manner as the LEA thinks appropriate;

- a duty to keep under review the arrangements made for special educational needs provision and, to the extent that it appears necessary or desirable for the purposes of co-ordinating provision for children with special educational needs, consult the Funding Agency for Schools, and the governing bodies of maintained, voluntary and grant-maintained schools;[49]

- a duty to have regard to the provisions of the Code of Practice on the Identification and Assessment of Special Educational Needs.[50]

Duties and powers of LEAs towards adults with learning difficulties and/or disabilities

197. The creation of the FEFC following the introduction of the Further and Higher Education Act 1992 did not end all LEAs' duties to provide further education to adults. In particular, duties under section 41 of the Education Act 1944 remain.

Functions of local education authorities in respect of further education

(1)   It shall be the duty of every local education authority to secure the provision for their area of adequate facilities for further education.

(2)   Subsection (1) above does not apply to education to which section 2(1) or 3(1) of the Further and Higher Education Act 1992 applies, but in respect of education to which section 3(1) of that Act applies a local education authority may –

(a)   secure the provision for their area of such facilities as appear to them to be appropriate for meeting the needs of the population of their area; and

(b)   do anything which appears to them to be necessary or expedient for the purposes of or in connection with such provision.

(3)   Subject to subsection (4) below and section 14(1) to (4) of the Further and Higher Education Act 1992, in this Act 'further education' means –

(a)   full-time and part-time education suitable to the requirements of persons over compulsory school age (including vocational, social, physical and recreational training); and

(b)   organized leisure-time occupation provided in connection with the provisions of such education.

(4)   In this Act 'further education' does not include higher education or secondary education.

(6)   A local education authority may secure the provision of further education for persons from other areas.

(7)   In exercising their functions under this section a local education authority shall have regard to any educational facilities provided by institutions within the higher education sector, and other bodies, which are provided for, or available for use by persons in, their area.

(8)   In exercising their functions under this section a local authority shall also have regard to the requirements of persons over compulsory school age who have learning difficulties.

Education Act 1944 Section 41

198. The effect of the section is to oblige[51] LEAs to provide full-time and part-time education suitable to the needs of persons over the age of 16 insofar as the FEFC is not already under a duty to provide such education. It would appear that the section is directed towards 'evening class' type provision. However, it is obviously not limited to that and it would appear from the wording of the section that LEAs still have a lingering duty to provide some form of full-time further education, the purpose and scope of which is unclear. The intention behind section 41 is obscure and the extent of the duties imposed on LEAs by it is uncertain.

199. In exercising their powers and duties under section 41, LEAs are required, to have regard to persons with 'learning difficulties'. This is further defined by section 41(11) as a person who:

•   has significantly greater difficulty in learning than the majority of persons of his age; or

•   has a disability which either prevents or hinders him from making use of facilities of a kind generally provided in pursuance of the duty under section 41(1) for persons of his age.

This definition, which was inserted by the Further and Higher Education Act (the 1992 Act) is almost identical to the definition of students or children with learning difficulties given in that Act and the 1993 Act. The same points made above[52] in relation to those definitions therefore apply by analogy. However, it is submitted that it is difficult to form a clear view of the second limb of the learning difficulty test where the meaning of LEAs' duties under section 41(1) and thus of 'facilities generally provided' is so unclear.

Overlap of duties of LEAs and the FEFC

200. The interaction of the duties of LEAs and the FEFC owed to students of 16 years old and over is complex and can be confusing. The intention has been that the

Duties and Powers

areas of responsibility of the two will interlock, so that there is no, or very little, overlap, and even more importantly, no gaps of non-provision which leave some students unsupported.

201. It is not clear that this has been achieved. There are two areas of particular uncertainty, which are the scope of an LEA's duty to provide further education under section 41 of the Education Act 1944 (the 1944 Act), and the responsibility for a child who has a statement of special educational needs when that child is over compulsory school age.

Section 41

202. The scheme of the 1992 Act was to transfer responsibility for further education from LEAs to the FEFC. It is therefore rather surprising to find that a duty for LEAs to provide further education remains. Section 41 of the 1944 Act is set out in full at paragraph 199. This section provides that LEAs must secure adequate provision of further education in their area. This duty is then restricted, as the Act states that it does not apply to further education to which section 2(1) or section (1) of the 1992 Act applies (ie, further education which the FEFC is under a duty to provide). The section then confers a power on LEAs to provide education to which section 3(1) of the 1992 Act applies. In exercising all of these functions an LEA must have regard to the requirements of those over compulsory school age with learning difficulties (it should be noted in passing that there is no upper age limit to those who must be considered).

203. The effect of all of this is as follows. LEAs cannot provide, under this section, any full-time education for 16–18 year olds. (The power to provide sixth form places in schools is conferred by section 8(1A) of the 1944 Act.)

204. LEAs must secure adequate facilities for part-time further education for those over compulsory school age, and full-time further education for those 19 and older, where that education is not a course mentioned in Schedule 2 to the 1992 Act.

205. LEAs may secure part-time further education for those over compulsory school age and full-time further education for those 19 and older where that education is provided by a course mentioned in Schedule 2 to the 1992 Act, but they do not have to do so.

206. Finally, further education is defined in the 1944 Act as full-time and part-time education suitable to the requirements of persons over compulsory school age (including vocational, social physical and recreational training) which is not secondary or higher education.

207. Although highly complex, (a complexity arising mainly from the poor definition and confusing use of the term 'further education') these provisions do appear to mesh properly with the provisions of the 1992 Act. The position is explained in table 1.

Duties and Powers

Table 1

Type of education/type of student	Non-schedule 2 full-time education	Schedule 2 full time education	Non-schedule 2 part-time education	Schedule 2 part-time education
Student 16–18 at a school mentioned in s.5(4) of the 1992 Act.	FEFC cannot fund, LEA can fund under s.8(1A) of the 1944 Act.	FEFC cannot fund, LEA can fund under s.8(1A) of the 1944 Act.	FEFC cannot fund, LEA must fund under s.41 of the 1944 Act.	FEFC cannot fund, LEA can fund under s.41 of the 1944 Act.
Student 16–18 at a school not mentioned in s.5(4) of the 1992 Act.	FEFC must* fund under s.2 and 5(4) of the 1992 Act, LEA can fund under s.8(1) of the 1944 Act.	FEFC must* fund under s.2 and 5(4) of the 1992 Act, LEA can fund under s.8(1) of the 1944 Act.	FEFC cannot fund, LEA must fund under s.41 of the 1944 Act.	FEFC must* fund under s.3(1) and 5(4) of the 1992 Act, LEA can fund under s.11 of the 1944 Act.
Student 16–18 at a sector college.	FEFC must fund under s.2 of the 1992 Act, LEA can fund under s.8(1A) but not under s.41 of the 1944 Act.	FEFC must fund under s.2 of the 1992 Act, LEA can fund under s.8(1A) but not under s.41 of the 1944 Act.	FEFC cannot fund, LEA must fund under s.41 of the 1944 Act.	FEFC must fund under s.3(1) of the 1992 Act, LEA can fund under s.41 of the 1944 Act, but need not.
Student 19+ at a school mentioned in s.5(4) of the 1992 Act.	FEFC cannot fund, LEA must fund under s.41 of the 1944 Act unless the student is completing a course of secondary education.	FEFC cannot fund, LEA may fund under s.41 of the 1994 Act unless the student is completing a course of secondary education.	FEFC cannot fund, LEA may fund under s.41 of the 1994 Act unless the student is completing a course of secondary education.	FEFC cannot fund, LEA may fund under s.41 of the 1994 Act unless the student is completing a course of secondary education.
Student 19+ at a school not mentioned in s.5(4) of the 1992 Act.	FEFC cannot fund, LEA must fund under s.41 of the 1944 Act.	FEFC must* fund under s.3(1) of the 1992 Act, LEA can fund under s.41 of the 1994 Act.	FEFC cannot fund, LEA must fund under s.41 of the 1944 Act.	FEFC must* fund under s.3(1) of the 1992 Act, LEA can fund under s.41 of the 1944 Act.
Student 19+ at a sector college.	FEFC cannot fund, LEA must fund under s.41 of the 1944 Act.	FEFC must fund under s.3(1) of the 1992 Act, LEA can fund under s.41 of the 1944 Act.	FEFC cannot fund, LEA must fund under s.41 of the 1944 Act.	FEFC must fund under s.3(1) of the 1992 Act, LEA can fund under s.41 of the 1944 Act.

Notes

(i) Sector college means any institution within the further or higher education sector.

(ii) 'Must fund' is shorthand for a duty to secure adequate or sufficient provision.

(iii) Must* is intended to draw attention to the fact that this duty applies only if facilities within the further or higher education sectors are inadequate (see s.4 of the 1992 Act).

(iv) The statement that LEAs can but need not fund education at schools for students over 16 is subject to their duties to secure provision for statemented pupils.

(v) The table as a whole applies only to students with learning difficulties.

(vi) 'Schools not mentioned in s.5(4) of the 1992 Act' are in general the specialist colleges catering for students with learning difficulties.

208. Thus, it can be seen that where difficulties arise it is not because there is a type of provision which cannot be funded, but rather that overlapping duties create scope for dispute as to which agency should fund provision. It is also clear that the shift in responsibility for funding which occurs if a student leaves a school and enters a college offers a powerful financial incentive to LEAs to encourage children to leave schools at 16.

209. Three points deserve to be highlighted. The first is that although section 41 of the 1944 Act (which was inserted in that Act by section 11 of the 1992 Act) states that LEAs are under no duty to secure full-time education for those aged 16 to 18, section 8(1A) of the 1944 Act confers a power to do so. This is a power which LEAs are under a duty to consider exercising.

210. It appears that adequate provision of non-schedule 2 education, which could be of great benefit to students with learning difficulties or disabilities as it could include a wide range of courses teaching, for example, social or physical skills, is in many cases not being made. The effect of this is that students are required to argue for an ever-wider meaning of what is a course within Schedule 2 when it may be that their efforts would be better directed against the defaulting LEA. In borderline cases it will not be clear whether it is the LEA or the FEFC which should fund a course, a state of uncertainty which works to no-one's advantage. Finally, an equivalent table showing the responsibility for funding students in general would look rather different, as the FEFC funding would be restricted to sector colleges. The shift in responsibility where students with learning difficulties are concerned is most unhelpful. If the FEFC's role is to fund the further education sector, then provision outside the sector should always be paid for by LEAs. If the FEFC's role is to fund further education, then the general restriction on whom they may fund should be removed. The present

hybrid situation appears to be evidence of a confusion over what exactly the FEFC's role is.

Statements

211. An important factor determining who has responsibility for funding provision is whether or not the child has a statement maintained by his LEA. All the while a statement is in force the LEA retains primary responsibility for the child. However, once a child is over compulsory school age his LEA will only be obliged to maintain his statement for as long as he remains a registered pupil at a school.

212. This is because of the definition of a 'child' for the purposes of LEAs' duties towards children with special educational needs which is set out in section 156(5) of the Education Act 1993. The definition is noteworthy because it is non-exhaustive. The term 'child' is stated to include any person who is under the age of 19 and is a registered pupil[53] at a school (ie, broadly, an educational institution not within the further or the higher education sectors).

213. It will be seen, however, that the definition of 'child' in the Education Acts has little significance in the context of an LEA's duties towards children with special educational needs. The relevant definition for these purposes is the definition of a child for whom an LEA is responsible. It is this definition which governs the scope of an LEA's duties towards children with special educational needs and it can be seen at once from a consideration of the definition of the expression given in section 165(3) of the Education Act 1993 (see paragraph 214 below) that the type of children to whom LEAs will have a duty goes far beyond children who are registered as a pupil at a school and indeed may include children of pre-school age (clearly not relevant for present purposes) and children who do not attend school at all.

214. Section 165(3) states that an LEA will be responsible for a child if:

- he is registered at a maintained or grant maintained school or a grant-maintained special school;[54]

- he is being educated at another type of school at the expense of the LEA in question or of the Funding Agency for Schools;

- he is otherwise registered at a school and has been brought to the attention of the LEA as having or probably having special educational needs;

- he is not registered at a school but is between the ages of two and 16 and has been brought to the attention of the LEA as having or probably having special educational needs.

215. The difficulty of overlapping responsibilities may seem to arise, however, when a student with a statement needs to attend a private school after the age of 16. Both the FEFC and LEAs would appear to have responsibilities towards such a student and the question of who is to fund naturally arises. The relative priority of these duties has recently been determined by the courts in the case of R v Dorset County Council and the FEFC ex parte Mark Goddard (by his father and next friend Paul Goddard) (1994). In this case Mr Justice Auld drew a distinction between the duties of the FEFC and LEAs in respect of students aged 16 to 19 with statements of special educational needs. The judge pointed out that LEAs had an unqualified duty to provide statemented education at a school[55] under the Education Act 1981 (and by analogy the Education Act 1993). He contrasted this to the FEFC's duties to provide for the needs of students with learning difficulties (and specifically the Council's section 4(3) duty in respect of education outside the FE sector) which under the terms of the 1992 Act[56] must be exercised 'with regard' to education provided by other parties such as LEAs. The judge held that the existence of this caveat to the FEFC's duties towards students with learning difficulties means that LEAs will always have the primary duty to fund and provide where

a child had a statement and was to be educated in a school.[57]

216. The primacy of LEAs' duties in this area is an important right for students with learning difficulties insofar as the statementing regime set out in the Education Act 1993 (and formerly the Education Act 1981) creates a more comprehensive panoply of rights than the 1992 Act. In particular, statemented students are protected by the detailed provisions of the Code of Practice on the Identification and Assessment of Special Educational Needs (see paragraphs 349 and 350). Statemented students also have access to a statutory appeals procedure (in the form of the Special Educational Needs Tribunal; see paragraph 60 above) under the 1993 Act in the event that an LEA amend or cease their statement. This tribunal procedure has no equivalent under this regime, where students must rely on the non-statutory internal appeals procedure of the FEFC in the event that they disagree with a decision of the Council. Incorporating a statutory right of appeal into legislation is one way in which the rights of students with learning difficulties in the FE sector might be strengthened.

217. Some LEAs have attempted to arrange matters so that children will cease to be registered pupils at a school after their sixteenth birthday. Such a policy was severely criticised in R v Dorset County Council exp. Goddard. As a result of that case, LEAs may now not lawfully take actions which would have the effect of ceasing a statement (for example, arranging matters so that a child ceases to be a registered pupil at a school) without going through the formal steps required when a decision is taken to cease the statement. (If the statement is not ceased, then LEAs are under a duty to secure provision for the student in question.) Whilst this should lead to greater openness, it has done nothing to alleviate the basic problem of considerations of whose budget will have to pay for provision playing a role in the decision as to what institution a student should attend.

218. It thus appears that there is not a problem of 'gaps' between the responsibilities of LEAs and the FEFC, but the problem is rather one of excessive overlap and uncertain boundaries leading to a lack of clarity as to who should pay for what. A first step towards removing such uncertainties might be publication of statements of policy by the agencies concerned, but it may be that a conclusive solution would require ministerial guidance, or even an amendment to Schedule 2 to the 1992 Act. It must also be said that the statutory provisions governing this area are of almost labyrinthine complexity, which is most unhelpful for authorities trying, in good faith, to determine what their duties are.

Duties of governing bodies of schools

219. The duties of governing bodies of schools towards children with learning difficulties are also set out in the 1993 Act and specifically in section 161(1):

A governing body must:

- do its best to secure that the necessary provision is made for any pupil who has special educational needs;

- secure that, where the 'responsible person' – the head teacher or the appropriate governor – has been informed by the LEA that a pupil has special educational needs, those needs are made known to all who are likely to teach him or her;

- ensure that teachers in the school are aware of the importance of identifying, and providing for, those pupils who have special educational needs;

- consult the LEA and/or, as appropriate, the Funding Agency for Schools and the governing bodies of other schools, when it seems to them necessary or desirable in the interests of co-ordinated special educational provision in the area as a whole;

- report annually to parents on the school's policy for pupils with special educational needs;

- ensure that all pupils with special educational needs join in school activities together with pupils who do not have special educational needs, so far as that is reasonably practical and compatible with the pupil receiving the necessary special educational provision, the efficient education of other children in the school and the efficient use of resources (section 161);

- have regard to this Code of Practice when carrying out their duties toward all pupils with special educational needs (section 157).

(Extracted from the Code of Practice)

Governing bodies, as well as LEAs also have a duty to 'have regard' to the Code of Practice.

Duties of the Funding Agency for Schools

220. Once 10% of secondary school pupils in the area of an LEA are in grant-maintained schools, the Funding Agency for Schools (FAS) will acquire duties to secure that sufficient school places in the area are available.[58] The FAS does not acquire a duty[59] to 'have regard' to the provisions of the Code of Practice and the need for securing special educational provisions for those pupils with special educational needs, as this applies only to functions under Part III of the Education Act 1993, and the FAS only has functions under Part I of that Act. However, in exercising its powers the FAS must have regard to the needs of pupils with special educational needs. This means that if a statemented child requires provision in the independent sector then the duty to arrange and fund this will fall upon the LEA. Section 6 of the Education (Miscellaneous Provisions) Act 1953 places a duty on LEAs to pay the 'whole fee payable in respect of the education provided' in pursuance of arrangements made by the LEA under the Education Act 1993.

Duties of the Office for Standards in Education

221. The Office for Standards in Education (OFSTED) was set up by the Education (Schools) Act 1992. It has a duty to monitor special educational needs provision in schools and to comment on schools' adherence to the Code of Practice and the implementation of schools' special educational needs policies (required to be published by 1 August 1995). This forms part of OFSTED's standard inspection duties. It also has duties to monitor adult education provided by LEAs under section 55 of the Further and Higher Education Act 1992.

The Code of Practice

222. The Code of Practice on the Identification and Assessment of Special Educational Needs has been drawn up by the Secretary of State for Education pursuant to the Secretary of State's duty to issue such a Code under the 1993 Act[60]. The Code is required to be, and has been, approved by resolution of both Houses of Parliament.[61] The aim of the Code is to give 'practical guidance' to LEAs, schools and other agencies towards the discharge of their duties towards children with special educational needs; and all those agencies or persons that play any role in the exercise of LEAs' duties towards children with special educational needs have a duty to 'have regard' to it. This includes local authority social services departments (SSDs), district health authorities (DHAs), governing bodies of schools, headteachers and teachers. The FEFC, insofar as it assists LEAs in the drawing up of transition plans[62] for children with statements who are aged 14 or over, is probably also covered by the duty to have regard to the provisions of the Code.

223. The duty of the FEFC to have regard to the needs of students with learning difficulties and/or disabilities is discussed in paragraphs 101 and 102 above and in terms of various agencies' duties to have regard to the Code of Practice, many of the same points may be made: that is, the Code is generally supposed to act as a guide and not a 'fetter' and strict adherence to every letter of its provisions is not required. This being said, it is an inevitable conclusion that by specifying what it considers to be good practice in such great depth, both the Department for Education and Parliament does expect LEAs, schools and others to pay detailed attention to its provisions. This is reflected in the House of Lords debate on the legal status of the Code which took place last spring. In the debate Baroness Blatch, the Education Minister, stated that the duty to have regard to the Code was 'no light duty' and it was also pointed out by a Lord of Appeal in Ordinary, Lord Simon of Glaisdale, that the Code did give rise to a legal duty and the onus was on those departing from its provisions to 'justify that departure'. The onus was to show that the alternative action adopted by the agency in question produced at least as beneficial results as would have been achieved from following the Code.[63]

224. Insofar as an LEA, school, DHA or any other person or agency is required to have regard to the provisions of the Code by section 157 of the 1993 Act, the Code does therefore create a legal duty to comply. The Code's requirements for collaboration between agencies are discussed in greater detail in paragraphs 352 and 353 below.

The European Union

225. The European Union (EU) has no specific duties towards students either with or without learning difficulties. However, the Treaty of European Union (otherwise known as the Maastricht Treaty)[64] gives the EU competence to develop common policies for educational and vocational training programmes.

226. This has resulted in the creation of the Leonardo da Vinci and Socrates programmes, which, although not specifically for students with learning difficulties, do contain

provisions for their benefit. The Leonardo programme, in particular, deals with community-wide vocational training measures and provides monies for encouraging specific vocational training measures for disadvantaged young people, including those with physical or mental disabilities. Some ECU 620 million have been earmarked for the programme for the period 1993–1999 and anybody involved in vocational training and, in particular, public authorities, training bodies or universities may apply for funding.

227. The Socrates programme has as its (somewhat vague) objective the establishment of co-operative educational programmes between universities, schools and other educational bodies in different member states. The Socrates programme expressly states that:

> [I]t is necessary to ensure that children and adolescents with disabilities are able to participate as fully as possible in the Socrates programme . . . The Community and member states should promote access, particularly for the less privileged, to the initiatives organised as part of the Socrates programme, thus actively combating social exclusion.

228. Funding is available for projects which, at least in part, aim to improve the level of achievement of all pupils and, in particular, the needs of children with specific educational needs and incapacities. Funding may also be available for exchanges of staff and to support partnerships and projects between schools. A sum of ECU 850 million has been earmarked for the Socrates programme over the period 1995–1999.

ENDNOTES

5   The scheme of the Education Acts 1944–1994 is that the FEFC should have the primary legal responsibility for the provision of full-time education suitable for the needs of people aged over 16 years. Local education authorities' legal duties to provide full-time education (broadly) only extend to pupils aged up to 16 (see section 8 Education Act 1944). LEAs have a power to provide full-time education suitable to the requirements of students in the 16 to 19 age range (section 8(1A) Education Act 1944 as inserted by section 10 of the Further and Higher Education Act 1992). No analogous legislative requirements apply to any body in respect of the provisions of higher education.

6   The 1992 Act gives no explanation of what is intended by the use of the different words 'adequate' and 'sufficient'. In the Commons debate on the 1992 Act Mr Timothy Eggar MP for the Government said that the intention behind the use of the 'adequate' /'sufficient' wording was to mirror the same terms used in section 8 (duty of LEAs to secure provision of primary and secondary schools) and section 41 (functions of LEAs in respect of further education) of the Education Act 1944. The intention of the Government was simply to try to carry forward these provisions in the same terms to the new funding councils. Mr Eggar stated 'we have deliberately sought to replicate the existing words so as not to send unintended messages as to the extent of the provisions and the duties that rest on the different parties . . . we have sought to the best of our drafting ability, to keep the status quo within the new provisions'. The relevant debate in the House of Lords shows that Parliament intended to confer a somewhat stronger duty by use of the word 'sufficient'.

7   Such education must be suitable for persons over the age of 16 (section 2).

8   Section 2(4) Further and Higher Education Act 1992.

9   These courses are listed in Schedule 2 to the 1992 Act and include courses designed to teach independent living skills to persons having learning difficulties and which prepare them for entry to another course on the list. Schedule 2 courses include basic literacy and numeracy courses, GCSE, GCE A level and AS level and vocational courses.

10   Section 3(3). The existence of these powers is a useful protection for the FEFC insofar as it will not be acting *ultra vires* if it provides a higher standard of provision than is strictly necessary under the 1992 Act.

11   A discussion of the definition of 'learning difficulty' is set out in paragraphs 103 to 114.

12   Section 4(2) 1992 Act.

13   Contrast this to the duty on various agencies to 'have regard' to the Code of Practice on the Identification and Assessment of Special Educational Needs in section 157 Education Act 1993.

14   R v Police Complaints Board exp. Madden [1983] 2AER 353

15   Ishak v Thowseek [1968] 1 WLR 1718 states that a duty to have regard to something does not necessarily impose a strict duty to comply with it.

16   Secretary of State for Education and Science v Tameside Metropolitan Borough Council [1977] AC 1014.

17   Associated Provincial Pictures House Ltd v Wednesbury Corporation [1948] IKB 223. The standard of reasonableness required by the Courts is not a high one. Courts are generally reluctant to label decision makers 'irrational' or 'perverse'. In Council for Civil Service Unions v Minister for the Civil Service [1985] AC, Lord Diplock defined the level of irrationality which would justify intervention by the courts as 'a decision which is so outrageous in its defiance of logic or of accepted moral standards that no sensible person who had applied his mind to the question to be decided could have arrived at it'. Judges are more likely to find grounds to intervene in other areas, eg, failing to act in accordance with the stated purpose therefore the relevant Act (Padfield v Minister of Agriculture, Fisheries and Food), taking irrelevant considerations into account or failing to take account of relevant considerations.

18 Certain parts of the section 156 definition of a child with a learning difficulty also refer to the learning difficulties of children under the age of 5, but these are irrelevant for present purposes.

19 And indeed those pre-school children covered by section 156(2)(c).

20 In R v Isle of Wight Council ex parte RS, CA [1993] 1 FLR 634 the Court of Appeal referred to the fact that estimates suggested one in five children had special educational needs and appeared to suggest that this was the number of children covered by the definition of learning difficulty.

21 This is also the policy of the Education Act 1993 (see section 160 of that Act).

22 See endtnote 6 above for the definition of 'adequacy' under the Education Acts. The duty to secure provision outside the FE sector where provision within the sector is inadequate is in contrast to the Council's duty under section 2 of the 1992 Act to make available sufficient full-time education to meet the reasonable needs of any person under the age of 19 requiring such provision. The question arises as to whether facilities could ever be inadequate where Council had complied with its duty to provide 'sufficient' facilities. It is submitted that, in fact, there is no conflict between the sections. Section 2 creates a general target duty for the FEFC in respect of its population as a whole and arguably is not intended to give rise to any rights for students as individuals. (R v ILEA ex parte Ali [1990]). By contrast section 4 of the 1992 Act gives rights to an identifiable class of students with specific needs and cannot in any sense be described as a general 'target' duty. It creates an individual right for each such student to receive provision according to his needs.

23 See paragraphs 120 and 121.

24 Section 4(3). As to the comparative responsibilities of LEAs and the FEFC in respect of statemented children over 16 years of age receiving education in independent schools; see paragraphs 30 and 31.

25 This is effectively all FE colleges funded by the FEFC.

26 The Council's powers with regard to provision outside the FE sector do not extend to providing for students at the following types of institutions:

– LEA-maintained schools;

– grant-maintained schools;

– city technology colleges;

– city colleges for the technology of the arts.

There is a direct prohibition on the Council funding education at these types of institutions. Provision for students with learning difficulties at these types of schools and colleges is governed by a separate regime under the Education Act 1993, which is discussed in paragraphs 194 *et seq.*

27 Compulsory school age is the lower cut-off point.

28 Section 4(3).

29 'Words must be interpreted as having their ordinary English meaning as applied to the subject matter with which they are dealing' per Graham J in Exxon Corporation v Exxon Insurance Consultants International Ltd [1981] 1 WLR 623 at 633.

30 Section 2(5) and 3(4), 1992 Act.

31 Sections 2(5) and 3(4) Further and Higher Education Act 1992. The 1992 Act gives no definition of what Parliament intended by the notion of proportionality of expenditure. In the House of Lords debate on this issue concern was expressed that use of the term might result in provision for students with 'special needs' being automatically classified as disproportionate expenditure. Lord Cavendish, for the Government, said that this was not so and that the meaning of the term was 'expenditure which is out of proportion to what is being provided'. This did not mean that the FEFC would not be required to avoid 'expensive' provision Lord Cavendish states that 'if the provision is proportionate to the need, even if it be expensive, this clause would not rule it out.' There is no threat here to students with disabilities.

32   Provided such college is providing full-time education suitable to the requirements of students of 16 to 19 years of age.

33   Published by the Department for Education, 1994. As to the provisions of the Code see paragraphs 222 to 224.

34   This is in any event part of a general requirement to monitor quality under section 9 of the 1992 Act.

35   See paragraph 15 above and endnote 6.

36   The Council has no express powers or duties under the Act to carry out quality checks on institutions outside the sector and to this extent it has no implied power to demand co-operation from independent colleges. However, section 54 of the Act requires the governing body of any institution which receives funding from the FEFC to provide the Council with such information as it may require for the purposes of the exercise of its functions. It might also be added that a college would be well advised to co-operate with any inspection by the Council if it wishes to continue to receive funding.

37   Persons over the age of 16 in the case of part-time education and persons over the age of 19 in the case of full-time education.

38   Citizen's Charter Unit, Cabinet Office, July 1994.

39   Central Office of Information, Informability Unit, November 1993.

40   A new definition of 'school' to apply throughout the Education Acts is given in section 14(5) of the Further and Higher Education Act 1992. This states that 'school' means any educational institution not within the further or higher education sector, which provides either primary education or secondary education or both. By virtue of section 14(5)(c) independent sixth form colleges providing FE courses for students up to the age of 19 are also now included in the definition of the word 'school'.

41   Part III of the 1993 Act (sections 156 to 191) concerns special educational needs.

42   Relevant provisions are also found in section 6, Education (Miscellaneous) Provisions Act 1953.

43   Specifically section 166; see paragraph 305.

44   For a discussion of this definition, see paragraphs 212 and 213.

45   See paragraph 103 *et seq.* for a discussion of this term.

46   For a discussion of the meaning of this term, see paragraph 107.

47   See paragraphs 109 to 114.

48   Schedule 10 of the Education Act 1993 sets out a detailed regime for involving parents in the statementing process and in the choice of school, including a right to make representations in relation to a proposed statement.

49   Section 159 Education Act 1993.

50   Section 157 Education Act 1993 (see paragraphs 222 to 224 for a discussion of the Code and the duty to 'have regard' to it).

51   LEAs also have a power to provide further education which the FEFC are under a duty to provide under section 3(1) of the 1992 Act.

52   See paragraph 113.

53   This means any person whose name has been entered in the admissions register of a school required to be kept by section 80 Education Act 1944. However, by virtue of section 14(6) of the Further and Higher Education Act 1992 (which defines the expression 'pupil') it cannot include a person for whom part-time education suitable to the requirements of persons over compulsory school age is being provided.

54   A 'special school' is a school specially organised to make special educational provision for pupils with special educational needs and which is approved by the Secretary of State for Education under section 188 of the 1993 Act (section 182, Education Act 1993).

55   In the Goddard case, Auld J held that LEAs had the primary legal duty 'for statemented provision in schools', which since the introduction of section 14(5) Further and Higher Education Act 1992 would include independent FE colleges. In practice, however,

the DFE and FEFC have held that LEAs should only be responsible for funding statemented education in secondary schools and that provision in independent FE colleges (legally 'schools') should be the responsibility of the FEFC. Funding allocations are made on the basis of this division of responsibility. It is the DFE's view (not shared by the authors of this report) that LEAs have no duty to fund statemented provision in independent FE colleges because the duty to fund special educational provision only applies where such provision is made in primary or secondary schools (section 6 Education (Miscellaneous Provisions) Act 1953. It is the authors' view that LEAs have an implied duty to fund special educational provision in all types of 'school'. This view is based on the fact that section 168 of the Education Act 1993 places a duty on LEAs to secure statemented provision in schools irrespective of type, as reflected Auld J's judgement in Goddard. It is submitted that it would be a nonsense for Parliament to have placed a duty on LEAs to secure provision which they did not also have a duty to fund.

56   See paragraph 117.

57   The same points apply by analogy to funding by the Funding Agency for Schools. However, in R v Oxfordshire County Council exp. P (1995) the court upheld the legality of a general policy (which was in fact subject to exceptions in a proper case) that all students post-16 should be educated in FE colleges. Inasmuch as this is the clear policy of the Education Acts themselves, this was not a surprising result. However, the LEA was held to have acted lawfully in discontinuing a student's statement (unlike Dorset, having followed a proper procedure) notwithstanding the fact that the facilities at the local FE college were not adequate for the student's needs. (It is not clear whether the LEA asked the Council to consider funding a placement outside the FE sector in this case.)

58   Section 12, Education Act 1993; DFE Circular 6/94. The Secretary of State must make an Order for this to apply.

59   Section 157(2), Education Act 1993.

60   Section 157(1), Education Act 1993.

61   Section 158(4), Education Act 1993.

62   See paragraph 352 below.

63   Hansard, H.L. Vol. 545, col 487.

64   Articles 126 and 127 of the Maastricht Treaty.

Transport

· ·

Introduction

229. The provision of free or subsidised transport may be made to a student with or without learning difficulties, just as transport may be made available to any other student. Although the enabling statutory provisions do not distinguish between disabled students or those with learning difficulties, the different needs of the disabled or those with learning difficulties can require extra provision to be made for such students. This section of the report describes the powers and duties governing the provision of transport.

230. The principal statutory provision governing transport services is section 55 of the Education Act 1944, which reads:

> (1)   A local education authority shall make such arrangements for the provision of transport and otherwise as they consider necessary or as the Secretary of State may direct for the purpose of facilitating the attendance of persons receiving education –
>
> (a)   at schools
>
> (b)   at any institution maintained or assisted by them which provides higher education or further education (or both)
>
> (c)   at any institution within the further education sector or
>
> (d)   any institution outside the further education sector and higher education sector, where a further education funding council has secured provision for those persons at the institution under section 4(3) of the Further and Higher Education Act 1992;
>
> and any transport provided in pursuance of such arrangements shall be provided free of charge.

231. There are thus two criteria which must be fulfilled before a student will be entitled to free transport from his or her LEA. The student must be receiving education at one of the specified types of institution, and the transport must be necessary to facilitate his attendance. The section does not say that this is attendance at the institution, so the section would appear to be apt to cover facilitating attendance at other sites if that was required by the education given at the institution itself. If these criteria are met then the LEA must provide free transport. It should be observed that the student's age does not play any direct part in governing his entitlement to free transport under this subsection, although indirectly it may be very important, as discussed below. However, unless it is clearly not the case, the discussion which follows relates to all students regardless of their age.

The specified institutions

232. There should be no difficulty in determining whether or not a student is attending an institution of the specified type. It is notable that an LEA can be under a duty to provide transport for students for whom it is under no duty to make any educational provision. For example, any student receiving education at a further education college could potentially be entitled to free transport, even though the tuition fees of such students would almost certainly be paid by the FEFC. Section 55(1)(d) set out at paragraph 230 above is a particularly clear example of this.

233. Thus at paragraph 76 of DFE Circular 1/93, it is stated that:

> *It continues to be a matter for the LEA to consider any arrangements necessary for the provision of transport*

· **53** *from home to college . . . This includes transport for students with learning difficulties who are attending colleges in the new further education sector, and such students who have been placed by the Further Education Funding Council in institutions outside the further and higher education sectors.*

234. The logic of imposing this duty on the LEA is no doubt that educational institutions or funding councils do not have the resources to maintain a fleet of vehicles to transport students, with the garages, maintenance facilities and staff which that would entail, whereas LEAs will have to arrange for transport for some of their schoolchildren and so they can fairly easily and cheaply provide transport for other students as well. It might be observed that in this era of the tendering of local authority services to private contractors, this justification is less strong than it has been in the past, as the institution (or, rather less plausibly, a funding council) could presumably make arrangements with private contractors in the same way that an LEA can.

235. 'Facilitating attendance' under the wording of section 55(1) of the Education Act 1944 appears to be sufficiently broad as to make it arguable that the LEA may be obliged to provide free transport between sites if the student is already in receipt of free transport between home and college. Otherwise the student would be unable to attend a proportion of his or her classes at the institution if they were located on a different site. It seems inevitable, however, that for this to be so then the inter-site transport must also be 'necessary' within the meaning of section 55(1), and this is unlikely often to be the case.

Necessary transport

236. When transport is necessary is clearly the central question when determining whether a student will be entitled to free transport. Although an LEA is entitled to form its own view as regards the scope of 'necessity', it is possible to give some guidance as to the kind of circumstances which will be likely to make transport a necessity.

237. Section 55(3) of the Education Act 1944 states that when an LEA is considering whether it is required to make arrangements under section 55(1) in respect of any particular person, it:

> . . . shall have regard (amongst other things) to the age of the person and the nature of the route, or alternative routes which he could reasonably be expected to take.

238. The age of the student and the nature of the route are therefore clearly relevant factors. As might be expected, the younger the student, and the more arduous the route, the more likely it is that transport will be necessary. Exactly what weight will be given to these factors is a matter for the LEA (within the limits on such discretions imposed by public law).

239. Although it is not expressly stated, the person's ability to take the route in question must also be relevant. A route which is suitable for an able-bodied person might be impassable or unreasonable for a disabled person. To take an extreme example, an able-bodied child would be able to take a route to school which required him to go up and down a flight of steps, but the same route would be impassable to a child in a wheelchair. Clearly transport could be necessary for the child using a wheelchair despite being unnecessary for the able-bodied child.

240. By similar reasoning it would seem that a person's mental abilities would be a factor which should be considered when determining whether it is necessary to provide him with transport.

241. However, it is clear that the test of when transport is necessary is a difficult one. The route to school must be extremely demanding before an LEA will be obliged to conclude that transport is necessary. Thus, for example, it is a defence for a parent

Duties and Powers

charged with failing to ensure the attendance of their child at school to say that it is not possible for the child to reach the school. Section 199(4) Education Act 1993 provides the statutory defence:

> The child shall not be taken to have failed to attend regularly at the school if the parent proves –
>
> (a) that the school at which the child is a registered pupil is not within walking distance of the child's home, . . .

At section 199(5) 'walking distance' is defined as:

> (a) in relation to a child who is under the age of eight years, two miles, and
>
> (b) in relation to a child who has attained the age of eight years, three miles.

242. It therefore appears that it would not inevitably be 'necessary' to provide transport to school for a nine-year-old child even if that child's daily journey to school required him to walk a six-mile round trip.

243. Distance is not the only factor in deciding whether transport is necessary. The difficulty of the route must also be considered. Once again, however, routes which a layman might regard as too difficult for a child to be expected to take have been approved by the courts as suitable. In Essex County Council v Rogers [1987] AC 66 the applicant was a girl aged 12. The applicant's parents had been convicted of failing to secure her attendance at school. The route specified by the LEA as being less than three miles involved her in crossing an unlit and partly unmade track which was isolated and dangerous to a child. It was also not always possible to use the path on the way home, even when it had been passable in the morning. It was difficult to use in winter. The House of Lords found that the route was available if a child could use it if accompanied as necessary. The presence of dangers on the route did not render the route unavailable. It may well be, however, in the light of continuing public concern over child safety, that this case is now not good law and should be confined to its own facts.

244. This case, and section 199(5), are clearly on a different point to the question of whether transport is necessary under section 55 of the Education Act 1944, but in the authors' view they nevertheless provide very considerable support for any LEA which wished to argue that transport was only necessary in the most extreme cases. Further support for this view can be found in the DFE Circular 1/93. Paragraph 108 states that:

> In practice, the Secretary of State would probably **consider it reasonable** for an LEA to decide that free transport would be necessary for a post-16 pupil or student only if he or she
>
> (i) was ordinarily resident in their area
>
> (ii) attended the nearest suitable school or college, even if it were in another LEA's area or was not the school or college considered appropriate by the LEA; and
>
> (iii) had special educational needs or learning difficulties or other individual circumstances which the LEA considered made free transport 'necessary'.
>
> (Authors' emphasis)

245. This paragraph contains some useful guidance, but it is notable that the paragraph does not state that the Secretary of State considers that transport would be necessary if conditions (i) to (iii) were satisfied, but merely that she probably would not consider such a conclusion unreasonable. The paragraph is also important in that it highlights special educational needs or learning difficulties (and, it is suggested, by necessary implication, disabilities) as a factor important in determining whether transport is necessary for an individual student.

246. A difficult question is whether the means of a student or his parents are relevant in considering whether transport is necessary. The significance of this is that under the Public Passenger Vehicles Act 1981, an LEA is empowered to carry students who do not fall within section 55(1) of the 1944 Act on the same bus as students who do qualify, and to charge a fee for so doing. Thus if finances were a relevant consideration an LEA would be able to argue that free transport was not necessary for a student, and then provide him with transport at a charge on the same vehicle that he would have travelled on for free if his parents were poorer.

247. There is no direct suggestion in the statute or in case law that finances are a relevant consideration. However, it has been held that other personal circumstances of the student's parents are relevant to deciding whether or not transport is necessary. In George v Devon County Council [1988] 3 WLR 1386, the fact that it was reasonably practicable for one of the child's parents to be available to accompany the child on his walk to and from school meant that it was not necessary to provide him with transport, as he could take a route to school which would have been too dangerous for the child alone. Can this be extended to the case where it is reasonably practicable for the parent to pay for transport?

248. The authors' view is that it cannot, and that the finances of the student or his parents are not relevant for the purposes of section 55(1). If this were not so, the effect would be that the LEA could charge to provide transport to those who could afford to pay, where that transport would otherwise be available free. This would appear to be a device to avoid the stipulation in section 55(1) that transport shall be provided free of charge, and thus it appears that finances should not be a relevant consideration.

249. An LEA's freedom to set whatever standard of necessity it chooses is, of course, somewhat limited. In some cases it could not reasonably be said that transport was not necessary. In addition, paragraph 111 of DFE Circular 1/93 reads in part:

The Secretary of State hopes that, in considering their use of their transport duties and powers, LEAs will have full regard to the possible effect of their policies on young people's willingness and ability to participate in education after the age of 16.

250. However, it is clear that LEAs have a fairly free hand to adopt either a relatively generous policy towards provision of free transport, or a restrictive policy.

Transport which is not 'necessary'

251. If it is not considered necessary to provide a student with free transport, an LEA is under no duty to provide the student with any assistance with transport. However, LEAs have a range of powers to help such students, and so some provision may be made for such students at the LEA's discretion. Section 55(2) of the Education Act 1944 reads as relevant:

A local authority may pay the whole or any part as the authority think fit of the reasonable travelling expenses of any person receiving education at any school or at any institution as is mentioned in subsection (1) above . . .

252. As paragraph 26 of the DFE letter of 21 January 1994 makes clear, the LEA's powers under section 55(2) do not extend to arranging or providing any transport, but only to providing financial assistance. Thus the student or his parents must actually arrange the transport themselves. This could present serious difficulties, for example in the case of a wheelchair-using student dependent on public transport, but it is submitted that students who could not make their own arrangements for transport should fall within section 55(1) in any case. The letter also states that the means of the parents

Duties and Powers

of the child may be considered in deciding whether or not to provide financial assistance.

253. Section 46(1) of the Public Passenger Vehicles Act 1981 allows an LEA to use a vehicle, when it is being used to provide free transport to students who qualify under section 55(1) of the 1944 Act, to carry as fare-paying passengers persons other than those for whom the free school transport is provided.

254. Under section 93(1) of the Transport Act 1985, local authorities outside Greater London have the power to establish schemes whereby certain categories including disabled people, children under 16, or young people aged between 16 and 18 and in full-time education can travel on public transport at concessionary rates:

> (1)   Any local authority or any two or more local authorities acting jointly may establish a travel concession scheme for the provision of travel concessions on journeys on public passenger transport services . . .
>
> (7)   The persons eligible to receive travel concessions under any such scheme are . . .
>
> (b)   persons whose age does not exceed sixteen years;
>
> (c)   persons whose age exceeds sixteen years but does not exceed eighteen years and who are undergoing full-time education;
>
> (d)   persons suffering from any disability or injury which, in the opinion of the authority or any of the authorities responsible for administration of the scheme, seriously impairs their ability to walk; . . .

255. Thus if a local authority outside Greater London puts such a policy in place it is able to provide reduced price transport for anyone under 16, and any student under 18 in full-time education, as well as people of any age who are disabled in such a way as to seriously impair their ability to walk. The disability is assessed by the local authority or any other authorities responsible for administering the scheme.

What is to be expected of the transport provided?

256. Section 55(1) requires the provision of 'transport and otherwise'. The words 'and otherwise' enable the LEA to provide staff to take care of the students on their journey, as well as the transport itself. Failure to provide such staff, where they are needed, will result in the LEA being liable for any injury caused to a student as a result. The standard of care to be taken by the LEA in seeing that the students are transported safely is that of the 'reasonably prudent parent applying his mind to school life'.

257. In the case of R v Hereford and Worcester County Council, ex parte P (1992) *The Times* 13 March, the applicant, who had Down's Syndrome, was provided with free transport. P's journey to and from school was extended owing to the minibus having to take a circuitous route in order to pick up and drop off two other children at their respective schools on the way. P was also strapped in for the whole of the one-hour journey. The journey door to door by the most direct route would take 30 minutes.

258. Section 55(1) of the Education Act 1944 was read as creating a duty to provide transport which conveyed the student to and from school safely and without undue stress and delay. Otherwise, the Court said the student 'will not benefit from the education offered at the school.' If the transport is not provided safely or it causes the student undue distress in the process, it is unlikely to be conducive to his or her education. These arrangements were not adequate to discharge the LEA's duty, because P was put under undue stress by them. The LEA had to rethink the transport it provided for P.

259. If the student is of an age to be statemented, then non-stressful transport was held to be a form of non-educational provision that should be specified in the statement.

Changes in policy

260. In the event that an LEA wishes to alter its transport policy, it should consider paragraph 113 of the DFE Circular 1/93 which states that the 'Secretary of State considers it desirable for LEAs to change their transport policies only at the beginning of an academic year.' The circular goes on to say that in the interest of fairness, an LEA should not make changes that would deprive a student of transport whilst he is in the course of his education at a particular institution. Thus, any changes of policy may have to be introduced gradually, taking care that the rights and expectations of students benefiting under the old policy are maintained.

Disputes

261. It is possible that the LEA and parents of the child in question may differ in their opinion of which school or college would best suit the needs of the student. In this case it may be that it is not necessary to provide transport to the LEA's preferred choice of school, but that transport will be required to facilitate attendance at the parents' choice. If the LEA agree to provide education at the school which is further away, must they also pay for transport to it?

262. Under the DFE Code of Practice on Special Educational Needs, it is for the LEA to decide where the student is to be educated. The Code goes on:

> *The school preferred by the parents may, in the event, be further away from the student's home than another school which is, in the opinion of the LEA, equally appropriate to the student's special educational needs. In such a case it would be open to the LEA to name the nearest school, because that would be compatible with the efficient use of the LEA's resources. It would also be open to the LEA to name the school preferred by the student's parents, **so long as the parents met the transport costs**.*

(Authors' emphasis)

263. <u>R v Essex County Council, ex parte C (1993)</u> *The Times* 9 December a child with special educational needs was statemented and the statement referred to a school within three miles of his home. His parents preferred another school at some 14 miles distance from his home. The statement made reference to this school and said that 'in accordance with the Authority's home-to-school transport policy, Mr and Mrs C will be responsible for all travelling expenses and arrangements.'

264. The parents applied for judicial review arguing that the LEA were under a duty to provide free transport. It was held that no such duty existed. The parental choice relieved the LEA from the duty to provide either transport or a place at a school within three miles of his home. Parental choice was not to be allowed to override the duty to avoid unreasonable public expenditure. The annual cost of transporting C to and from the school of his parents' choice would be £4,000. This would be an unreasonable expense, as a closer (and equally appropriate, in the eyes of the LEA) school existed.

Other agencies

265. The LEA is the agency with primary responsibility for transport costs, in the educational context, but additional duties may arise for other agencies. For example, the local authority social services department may be required to pay for the provision of transport which a disabled person needs to facilitate his or her attendance at recreational or other facilities provided under section 29(1) of the National Assistance Act 1948 or to any similar facilities not in fact provided under that section (for example a day-centre run by a charity rather than a local authority). (Section 29(1) empowers local authorities to make arrangements to promote the welfare of people over 18 who have a one or more of a very wide range of disabilities or disadvantages either physical or mental.

It confers a wide power, and the facilities to which transport can be provided are accordingly wide.) These sections are broad enough to empower local authority social services departments to provide the range of transport services which they do in fact make available. Transport to educational facilities could certainly be provided under this power.

Social Services

Duties of local authority social services departments under the Children Act 1989 towards 'children in need' aged under 18

266. For young people under the age of 18 the flagship of the various welfare enactments is the Children Act 1989 (the 1989 Act). This Act places the onus of ensuring the welfare of 'children in need' on local authority social services departments (SSDs) and specifically section 17(1) of the 1989 Act places a general duty on SSDs to 'safeguard and promote' the welfare of such children.

(1) It shall be the general duty of every local authority (in addition to the other duties imposed on them by this Part):

(a) to safeguard and promote the welfare of children within their area who are in need; and

(b) so far as is consistent with that duty, to promote the upbringing of such children by their families;

by providing a range and level of services appropriate to those children's needs.

(2) For the purpose principally of facilitating the discharge of their general duty under this section, every local authority shall have the specific duties and powers set out in Part I of Schedule 2.

Children Act 1989 Section 17(1)

267. This section 17(1) duty is expressed in the broadest of terms. In particular, legally, the concept of the welfare of a 'child' is a wide one[65] embracing physical, emotional, moral and religious factors. Within these broad parameters what constitutes a child's welfare is a matter for the reasonable discretion of SSDs, which in the absence of a default, will usually not be subject to review by a court. This being said, the wording of the 1989 Act expressly requires that in every exercise of a local authority's discretion concerning a child's welfare, the authority must take into consideration the importance of promoting the welfare of the child within his or her own family (unless this is itself inconsistent with the child's welfare).[66]

268. More specific duties and powers of SSDs in respect of children in need are given in Schedule 2 of the Act. As will be seen below not all children who have learning difficulties will fall within the definition of children 'in need' and therefore only those duties and powers set out in Part 1 of Schedule 2 which can generally be expected to apply to students with learning difficulties and/or disabilities in the relevant age group are set out in table 2. Insofar as a student's learning difficulty arises from emotional problems relating to his home circumstances, the 1989 Act contains a host of duties and powers enabling SSDs to take action to protect the student and if necessary to take him into care. No attempt has been made to repeat all these provisions here.

Table 2

Legislative source	Duty or power	Action
Section 17(2), Schedule 2, paragraph 1(1)	Duty	to take reasonable steps to identify the extent to which there are children 'in need' in their area
Section 17(2), Schedule 2, paragraph 1(2)(a)	Duty	to publish information about services provided by LAs under the Children Act[67] and where the LA considers it appropriate about related services provided by others
Section 17(2), Schedule 2, paragraph 1(2)(b)	Duty	to take reasonably practicable steps to ensure that those people in their area who might benefit from the services being offered receive the information published
Section 17(2), Schedule 2, paragraph 2	Duty	to maintain a register of disabled children
Section 17(2), Schedule 2, paragraph 3	Power	to assess the needs of a child in need for the purposes of the Children Act at the same time as an assessment under the Chronically Sick and Disabled Persons Act 1970, the Education Act 1993, the Disabled Persons (Services, Consultation and Representation) Act 1986, or any other Act
Section 17(2), Schedule 2, paragraph 6	Duty	to provide services for disabled children to give them as normal a life as possible and to minimise the effect of their disabilities
Section 17(2), Schedule 2, paragraph 8	Duty	to make such provision as they consider appropriate for children living with their families to receive advice, guidance and counselling, occupational, social or recreational activities, home help (including laundry facilities), travel and to have a holiday (with the child's family)
Section 17(2), Schedule 2, paragraph 9	Duty	to provide such family centres as the LA considers appropriate where children and their families can receive counselling

269. SSDs also have duties under section 20 of the 1989 Act to provide residential accommodation for any child in need within their area, broadly:

- where his parents cannot or will not look after him;
- who has reached the age of 16 and whose welfare is likely to be seriously prejudiced if the authority does not provide him with such accommodation.

270. It will be seen from table 2 that local authorities have a power to carry out assessments to ascertain what services may be required by children in need in their area. This is strengthened into an effective duty by the relevant guidance[68] which states that 'SSDs will need to develop clear assessment procedures for children in need within agreed criteria which take account of the child's and family's needs and preferences,

racial and ethnic origins, their culture, religion and any special needs relating to the circumstances of individual families. The assessment procedures are not laid down in primary legislation or regulations but assessments under the 1989 Act should be undertaken in the context of Part 3[69] and Schedule 2 of the Act'.

271. It is to be noted that although the guidance relating to the 1989 Act issued by the Secretary of State for Health is officially described as guidance, the legal obligation to comply with it is quite as strong as the obligation on relevant agencies to have regard to the Code of Practice on the Identification and Assessment of Special Educational Needs. This is because under section 7 of the Local Government Social Services Act 1970, local authorities, in the exercise of their social services functions have a duty to act in accordance with general guidance from the Secretary of State.

Definition of a 'child' in the Children Act 1989

272. The scope of the duties of SSDs under the Children Act 1989 is governed, at least in part, by the definition of 'children' which is given in section 105(1) of the Act and is stated to mean any person who is under the age of 18.[70] This is clearly a much narrower definition than that given in those sections of the Education Act 1993 which deal with LEA's obligations towards children with special educational needs. It will be recalled that in this context, a 'child' is defined to include any person who has not yet attained the age of 19 and is a registered pupil at a school. In terms of the age ranges covered, the 1989 Act definition also stops substantially short of the FEFC's duties towards students with learning difficulties, which as a minimum extend to age 25 and in certain cases are not limited as to age in any way (see paragraph 97 above).

273. As the legislative regime dealing with students' education offers special treatment up to the age of 19 and in some cases even longer, it is questionable whether it is desirable to cut off the protection offered by the 1989 Act at age 18 when many young persons will still be in school or college. Although the National Assistance Act 1948 (see paragraph 282 below) contains many similar provisions to the 1989 Act, it cannot be said to offer the same degree of protection as the 1989 Act particularly to those young people with learning difficulties who suffer from emotional problems caused by their home circumstances rather than physical disabilities. This is particularly true in relation to the duties placed on local authorities to provide accommodation under section 20 of the 1989 Act, as there is no equivalent duty on SSDs to provide accommodation for young people aged over 18. In the interests of minimising disruption to a young person's education the question must be raised as to whether it would be desirable to extend the 1989 Act provisions beyond the age of 18 to those students still at school or further education college after this date until the date of their leaving full-time education or attaining the age of 19, whichever is the later.

Definition of a 'child in need'

274. As stated above, not all students who have learning difficulties and/or disabilities will fall within the definition of 'children in need'. This term is defined by section 17(10) of the Children Act 1989 and means, broadly, a 'child':

- who is unlikely to achieve or maintain a reasonable standard of health or development if the local authority do not provide services for him;

- whose health or development is likely to be significantly impaired or further impaired without those services; or

- who is disabled.

Definition of 'disabled' in the Children Act 1989

275. It is notable that a young person under 18 years old will automatically fall within the definition of a 'child in need' if he is 'disabled'. In turn, a child will be 'disabled'[71] if he or she meets any of the criteria listed in section 17(11) of the 1989 Act, that is, if he is:

- blind, deaf or dumb; or

- suffers from mental disorder[72] of any kind;

- is substantially and permanently handicapped[73] by illness, injury or congenital deformity or such other disability as may be prescribed.[74]

This definition exactly reflects the definition of 'disabled person' given in the National Assistance Act 1948 in respect of persons over the age of 18. Therefore if a child qualifies as a disabled person before the age of 18 then unless there is some change in his condition he will still be eligible to receive services after the age of 18 as well.

276. No indication is given in the 1989 Act as to how the various criteria for qualification as 'disabled' should be interpreted.[75] This is also true of the related guidance which suggests that in identifying disabled young persons, SSDs should 'liaise with their health and education counterparts to achieve an understanding of disability which permits early identification'. The guidance also goes on to suggest that a joint register of children with disabilities should be created between health, education and social services.

277. Perhaps the clearest guidance as to what constitutes disability in terms of both sensory impairment or physical disabilities is given in Part 3 of the Code of Practice on the Identification and Assessment of Special Educational Needs. As an example, the advice set out in the Code on detecting children with visual difficulties is:

Visual difficulties take many forms with widely differing implications for a child's education. They range from relatively minor and remediable conditions to total blindness. Some children are born blind; others lose their sight, partially or completely, as a result of accidents or illness. In some cases visual impairment is one aspect of multiple disability. Whatever the cause of the child's visual impairment, the major issue in identifying and assessing the child's special educational needs will relate to the degree and nature of functional vision, partial sight or blindness and the child's ability to adapt socially and physiologically as well as to progress in an educational context.

Paragraph 3:81 – Code of Practice on the Identification and Assessment of Special Educational Needs

It is submitted that it would be helpful if analogous criteria set out in new general guidance could be used in the field of social services.

278. General guidance on the interpretation by SSDs of disability under the 1989 Act would also help to promote consistent application of the Act's principles. In the education field, the Government's view has been that consistent application of principles by LEAs etc, is an end in itself.[76] However, it is not clear to what extent the provisions of the Code of Practice giving guidance on how to identify children who are disabled could simply be transferred across to the 1989 Act guidance. For example, it is not clear to what extent children whose special educational needs are provided for at school without the need for a statement would fall within the definition of 'disabled' in the 1989 Act. Likewise it is not clear to what extent students who have a learning difficulty under section 4(6) of the Further and Higher Education Act 1992 should or would be covered by the 1989 Act definition.

The definition of 'development'

279. The Children Act 1989 also states that a child will be 'in need' if:

- he is unlikely to achieve or maintain a reasonable standard of health or development without the provision for him of services by a local authority under the Act; or

- his health or development is likely to be significantly impaired without the provision for him of such services.

It is notable that these definitions go beyond those of 'learning difficulty' set out in the Education Acts in that they have a preventative as well as a corrective purpose.[77] They are designed to catch intellectual, behavioural or physical difficulties before these occur. It is questionable whether the definitions of learning difficulties in the Education Acts could be extended to cover students who might potentially acquire such learning difficulties.

280. Somewhat unusually perhaps, the 1989 Act does provide some guidance as to what Parliament intends the terms 'health' and 'development' to mean. 'Development' is expressed[78] to mean the 'physical, intellectual, emotional, social or behavioural development' of the child. There is no case law to shed further light on the term and once again it is for SSDs to exercise reasonable discretion in interpreting the scope of their duties.

281. 'Health' is defined by the 1989 Act as referring to either physical or mental health. In relation to provisions contained in a later section of the 1989 Act,[79] case law and guidance suggest that to assess the health of a child it is necessary to compare the child in question's health to that of a 'hypothetical similar child'. The standard of health therefore required by the 1989 Act to be safeguarded by SSDs is not the best possible health, but the standard of health that could reasonably be expected from such a child.

Duties under the National Assistance Act 1948 towards people over the age of 18

282. As 'children in need' reach their eighteenth birthday, the duties of SSDs towards them are no longer governed by the Children Act 1989 but instead by the National Assistance Act 1948 (the 1948 Act) and the Chronically Sick and Disabled Persons Act 1970 (the 1970 Act).[80] The 1948 Act, dealing as it does exclusively with the functions of SSDs towards adults, offers a less comprehensive regime in terms of the obligations of SSDs towards disabled persons.

283. The principal powers and duties created by the 1948 Act (and still in existence today) are as follows:

- a power to be exercised with the approval of the Secretary of State and a duty to such extent as the Secretary of State may direct,[81] to make arrangements for the provision of residential accommodation for persons who by reason of age, illness or disability[82] or any other circumstances are in need of care and attention which would otherwise not be available to them. SSDs are obliged to limit section 21 schemes to those approved by the Secretary of State (generally by circular) by virtue of the wording of section 21 itself and their broader duty to act in accordance with guidance issued by the Secretary of State;[83]

(1) Subject to and in accordance with the provisions of this Part of this Act, a local authority may with the approval of the Secretary of State, and to such extent as he may direct shall, make arrangements for providing:

(a) residential accommodation for persons aged eighteen or over who by reason of age, illness, disability or any other circumstances are in need of care and attention which is not otherwise available to them;

(b) . . .

(2) In making any such arrangements a local authority shall have regard to the welfare of all persons for whom accommodation is provided, and in particular to the need for providing accommodation of different descriptions suited to different descriptions of such persons as are mentioned in the last foregoing subsection.

Section 21, National Assistance Act 1948

- if accommodation is being provided under section 21 SSDs also have powers to provide transport to and from such accommodation and to make arrangements for the provision on the premises of other services which the local authority consider to be required;
- a duty to charge at a standard rate[84] for all such accommodation but taking into account ability to pay;
- powers in respect of disabled persons only[85] to make arrangements[86] to do any of the following acts:

  - informing disabled persons of the services available to them;
  - teaching disabled persons how to overcome the effects of their disabilities;
  - providing workshops for disabled people and related accommodation[87];
  - providing suitable work for disabled persons;
  - helping disabled persons dispose of the produce from their work;
  - providing recreational facilities.

Duties under the Chronically Sick and Disabled Persons Act 1970

284. SSDs' powers in the 1948 Act are extended and supplemented by the Chronically Sick and Disabled Persons Act 1970 (the 1970 Act),[88] which places a duty on local authorities to make arrangements for providing practical assistance for persons ordinarily resident in their area.[89] The facilities that may be provided by local authorities under section 2 are:

- practical assistance in the home;
- wireless, television, library facilities;
- lectures, games, outings;
- transport to and from place where services provided;
- adaptations or additional facilities in the home;
- holidays;
- meals (at home or elsewhere);
- telephones and special equipment.

Section 2(1) – Chronically Sick and Disabled Persons Act

A local authority has a duty to carry out an assessment of the needs of a disabled person to receive services under this section whenever requested to do so by a disabled person, his authorised representative or carer.[90]

285. The 1970 Act[91] also places various duties on local authorities to inform themselves of the number of persons in their area who might need services under section 29 of the National Assistance Act 1948 and to publish information about the services offered.

Definition of 'disability' in the National Assistance Act 1948 and the Chronically Sick and Disabled Persons Act 1970

286. Those persons who are to benefit from the welfare services set out above[92] and the 1970 Act are listed in section 29 of the 1948 Act. It is to be noted that the same list of persons is used to define a 'disabled' child under the Children Act and therefore an 18 year-old disabled young person who is passing from one regime to other should be confident that he will qualify for services under both. A more detailed analysis of the terms used is given in paragraph 275 *et seqq.* above in terms of the Children Act 1989 and the same points apply by analogy.[93]

287. It is important to note that the list of persons set out in section 29 of the 1948 Act

and cross-referred to determine local authorities' welfare duties under the 1970 Act includes only persons over the age of 18. This does not appear to have been taken on board by the authors of Volume 6 of the Children Act guidance (entitled Children with Disabilities)[94] which states that the 1970 Act 'imposes various duties upon local authorities towards disabled persons of all ages, including disabled children . . .' and then goes on to list sections 1 and 2 as being the relevant sections. This would appear to be an error in the guidance, although not significant in practice as all these facilities could be provided to disabled children under the general duty to promote their welfare under section 17(1) Children Act 1989.

Other Acts placing obligations on social services departments towards disabled people

288. Further powers and duties to provide 'care in the community' services to people with disabilities are given in the following acts:

- the National Health Service Act 1977 (NHS Act 1977);

- the National Health Service and Community Care Act 1990;

- section 117 of the Mental Health Act 1983;

- the Disabled Persons (Services, Consultation and Representation) Act 1986.

The National Health Service Act 1977

289. Under the National Health Service Act 1977 (NHS Act 1977)[95] local social service authorities have a duty to provide home help facilities (or to arrange for such provision) on an adequate scale for households where such help is required owing to the presence of a person suffering from illness or, amongst other things, handicapped as a result of having suffered from illness or by congenital deformity. Local authorities are also given a power to provide laundry facilities for households who are also being provided with

home help. Schedule 8[96] powers and duties for local authorities are in addition to separate duties in the Children Act 1989 concerning the provision of home help and laundry services to children under the age of 18.[97]

290. The list of persons who qualify to receive home help under the NHS Act 1977 is shorter but broader in application than that given in section 29 of the National Assistance Act or in the definition of a disabled child set out in the Children Act 1989 (see paragraph 275). This is understandable. The aim of the NHS Act 1977 is to assist those who need help whether on a short-term or long-term basis, for example, by providing temporary help for those recovering from an operation or an illness or by providing long-term support for the chronically ill and disabled, rather than to create a permanent entitlement. It may also be the case, in view of the limited nature of the duty imposed by section 21, that there is no practical need for a detailed definition to be given.

The Mental Health Act 1983

291. Under the Mental Health Act 1983[98] district health authorities (DHAs) are under a duty together with local social services authorities to provide, in co-operation with relevant voluntary agencies, after-care services for any such person on his or her ceasing to be detained in hospital and returning home until both the SSD and the DHA are satisfied that the person concerned no longer requires such services.

292. These provisions of the Mental Health Act will only apply to students with special learning difficulties and/or disabilities in the rare circumstances where a young person has been detained at a hospital under the 1983 Act because he or she is suffering from a mental illness or disorder etc, and, broadly, it is necessary for his or her own health and safety or for the protection of other persons that he should receive treatment in a hospital.

The NHS and Community Care Act 1990

293. The only pertinent provision in this Act for present purposes is the duty on SSDs to carry out assessments[99] of the needs of any person, when it appears to that local authority that that person may be in need of any community care services. For these purposes 'community care services' means services under the National Assistance Act (see paragraphs 282–283), the NHS Act 1977 (see paragraphs 289–290) and section 117 of the Mental Health Act 1983 (see paragraphs 291 to 292).

294. In carrying out their assessment of a person's needs for community care services, if the local authority finds that a person is 'disabled', there will be a duty on that authority to proceed automatically to decide what services that person requires[100] under the Chronically Sick and Disabled Persons Act 1970 (see paragraphs 284 and 285) and to inform the person of his rights under the Disabled Persons (Services, Consultation and Representation) Act 1986 (the Disabled Persons Act; see paragraphs 295 to 300). The definition of 'disabled person' in the 1990 Act is the same as that given in the Disabled Persons Act 1986 (see paragraph 300).

The Disabled Persons (Services, Consultation and Representation) Act 1986

295. The Disabled Persons (Services, Consultation and Representation) Act 1986 (the 1986 Act), to the extent that it has been introduced, is a key element in the statutory regime protecting disabled persons and is one of the central pieces of legislation that deal with the transition of a young person from full-time education to the outside world.

296. Particularly relevant to disabled students is section 5 of the 1986 Act. This places a duty on local education authorities in circumstances where they maintain a statement in respect of a student to form an opinion by means of an assessment as to whether that student is a 'disabled person' at certain stages of his school career.

297. Where as a result of such an assessment,[101] a local education authority has reached a decision that a young person is disabled and it subsequently appears to the responsible authority[102] that he will soon be leaving full-time education then the responsible authority is required to notify the SSD who must then carry out a further assessment of the needs of that person to determine what services should be provided by the local authority under any of the welfare legislation. The assessment is optional insofar as a student who is aged over 16 can decline to be assessed or, if he is under 16 years old, his parent or someone with parental responsibility has declined for him.

298. The 1986 Act[103] also places duties on SSDs in respect of patients with mental disorders who are to be released from hospital (including those detained under the Mental Health Act 1983) when they receive notification from those hospitals of the date of discharge. These duties involve assessing the patient's needs for the provision of welfare services after discharge and the provision of aftercare.

299. It is interesting to note that the early sections[104] of the 1986 Act have, at the time of writing, not yet been introduced. The reasons for this are not entirely clear but would appear to relate to the resource and administrative implications for local authorities of introducing the sections.[105] The sections in question were intended to give disabled persons the right to appoint an 'authorised representative' to represent their interests to local authorities on questions relating to provisions of welfare services.

Definition of 'disabled' in the Disabled Persons Act 1986

300. As is logical this definition is stated to be the same as in the Children Act 1989 for the purpose of young people under the age of 18 and the same as in the National Assistance Act (section 29) for persons over the age of 18. At present these two definitions are the same.

Community Care Charters

301. As for the Charter for Further Education (discussed at paragraph 190 *et seqq*.), Community Care Charters are not legally binding and do not give rise to legal rights but are a statement of a commitment to achieve a standard of service. Community Care Charters are drawn up on a local basis jointly between local authority housing departments, SSDs and the NHS and their priorities are to be determined locally but within an overall framework requirement.[106]

ENDNOTES

65   Case law suggests that the concept of 'welfare' must be understood in its widest sense and ought not to mean financial well-being or physical comfort only. In a New Zealand case <u>Walker v Walker and Harrison [1981]</u> cited by the England and Wales Law Commission in its Working Paper No. 96, welfare was defined as 'an all-encompassing word. It includes material welfare, both in the sense of adequacy of resources to provide a pleasant home and a comfortable standard of living, and in the sense of adequacy of care to ensure that good health and due personal pride are maintained. However, whilst material considerations have their place they are secondary matters. More important are the stability and security, the loving and understanding care and guidance, the warm and compassionate relationship, that are essential to the full development of the child's own character, personality and talent'. Section 1(3) Children Act also sets out a list of factors relating to a child's welfare which a court should take into account in the course of family proceedings. This list can also be used to inform social services departments' decisions as to what Parliament considers is likely to be for a child's welfare.

66   Section 17(1)(b), Children Act 1989. The Lord Chancellor emphasised the importance attached by Parliament to the upbringing of children within their own families in a debate during the committee stages of the Children Bill in the House of Lords: 'The idea is to ensure that so far as possible children are kept with their families . . . The real object of promotion is the upbringing of children who are in need by their families. It is only in so far as it is necessary to safeguard and promote the welfare of the children within the [local authority's] area who are in need that anything else needs to happen'. (502 HL Official Report 1287, 20 December 1988).

67   This duty relates only to section 17 (general duty to promote welfare of children in need), section 18 (day-care for pre-school and other children not yet attending school), section

20 (provision of accommodation for children generally).

68   The Children Act 1989 Guidance and Regulations, Vol. 6 Children with Disabilities, DoH 1991.

69   Part III of the Children Act (commencing with section 17) deals with welfare of children in need.

70   This definition is subject to paragraph 16(1) of Schedule 1 of the Act which deals with financial provision for children, ie, maintenance payments etc. The paragraph extends the definition of 'child' to include any person who has reached the age of 18 and in respect of whom an order for financial relief has been made. This extension of the definition of child only applies to matters covered by Schedule 1 of the Act and therefore does not affect matters dealt with by this report.

71   This is the same definition as is used in the Disabled Persons (Services, Consultation and Representation) Act 1986 in respect of the application of that Act to young people under the age of 18.

72   See the definition of this term in the Mental Health Act 1983, section 1 of which says that 'mental disorder' means mental illness, arrested or incomplete development of mind, psychopathic disorder and any other disorder or disability of mind.

73   There is no case law on what is meant by 'substantially and permanently' in the context of either the National Assistance Act 1948 or the Children Act. However, case law surrounding the use of the term 'substantially impaired' in section 2(1) Homicide Act 1957 states that substantial does not mean 'trivial or minimal, neither does it mean total. It is for the jury to decide whether the impairment is substantial' <u>(R v Lloyd [1967] 1 QB 175)</u>. In the absence of a jury it is to be deduced that local authority social services departments have been given a discretion as to how to interpret the section, which as discussed on previous occasions they should exercise reasonably and with regard only to relevant factors.

74   To date, no regulations have been made to extend the definition of a 'disabled person' under this section.

75   Case law is of limited assistance in determining how any of these terms are to be interpreted. The only case which appears to be in any sense relevant concerns the definition of the words 'blind'. In Henry Charles Christian v Samuel Tawiah Intiful [1954] the Privy Council giving judgement on a Commonwealth case stated that someone whose sight was impaired was not necessarily blind although being unable to read because of such impairment would constitute blindness. Of more relevance is the definition given in section 64 of the National Assistance Act 1948 which states that a blind person 'means a person so blind as to be unable to perform any work for which eyesight is essential'. It must be presumed in all cases that sight defects fully rectifiable by the use of glasses or contact lenses do not constitute blindness.

76   The Code is intended to 'ensure greater consistency in the making of statements' per Baroness Blatch, Minister for Education in the House of Lords debate on the Code. (Hansard, H.L. Vol. 54 columns 478 to 486).

77   The only analogous provisions are found in section 156(2)(c) Education Act 1993 which says that a child will have a learning difficulty if he is under 5 and, unless special educational provision is made for him, would be likely to fall under one of the two other heads defining children with a learning difficulty.

78   Section 17(11).

79   Section 31.

80   Specifically Part III of the National Assistance Act 1948. This Act which has been substantially amended since it was originally enacted was introduced to replace the old Poor Law. Section 1 of the 1948 Act which still remains repealed the Poor Law Act 1930.

81   Both power and duty are found in section 21 of the 1948 Act (as amended).

82   The term is not defined, but presumably could be construed as referring to those persons listed in section 29 of the 1948 Act (see paragraphs 275 et seq. and 286).

83   Under section 7, Local Authority Social Services Act 1970.

84   This standard rate is required to cover the full cost of the accommodation (section 22).

85   Section 29 National Assistance Act 1948.

86   LAs may also use a voluntary organisation or a private business to provide services under section 29 (section 30 National Assistance Act 1948).

87   Such accommodation is treated as if it were made under section 21 for the purposes of the LA making charges in respect of its provision (section 67(2) NHS and Community Care Act 1990).

88   Section 2.

89   Who are disabled within the meaning of section 29 of the 1948 Act.

90   Section 4, Disabled Persons (Services, Consultation & Representation) Act 1986.

91   Section 1.

92   Not including residential accommodation under section 21 of the 1948 Act.

93   It should be noted that the Secretary of State has powers under the Chronically Sick and Disabled Persons Act 1970 to extend or change the definition of 'disabled person' by order. To date this power has not been exercised. The Secretary of State has also not used his power under section 29 of the 1948 Act to extend the range of disabilities which covered by this section (and analogously no extensions have been made to the list of disabilities set out in section 17(11) of the Children Act).

94   Department of Health, HMSO 1991.

95   Section 21, paragraph 3, Schedule 8.

96   Schedule 8 also gives powers to local social services authorities to make arrangements for the provision of care and after care of persons with illnesses irrespective of age (paragraph 2, Schedule 8).

97   Section 17(2) and paragraph 8, Schedule 2 of the Children Act 1989 create a duty for SSDs to provide home help (which may include laundry facilities) to children in need where the SSD considers it to be appropriate.

98   Section 117.

99   Section 47 NHS and Community Care Act 1990.

100   As is required by section 4 of the Disabled Persons (Services, Consultation and Representation) Act 1986.

101   Assessments are carried out under this section and notifications received by an 'appropriate officer' of the LEA appointed specifically for the purposes of this section.

102   This expression is defined by section 5(9) and means:

(a)   in relation to a child at school, means the local education authority who are responsible for the child for the purposes of Part III of the Education Act 1993;

(b)   in relation to a person receiving full-time further or higher education an institution within the further education sector or the higher education sector, means the governing body of that institution; and

(c)   in relation to a person for whom a further education funding council has secured full-time education at an institution (other than a school) outside the further education sector or the higher education sector, the council.

103   Section 7. Analogous duties apply to HAs; see paragraph 99.

104   Sections 1 to 3.

105   In the relevant parliamentary debate, the Minister for Health stated 'I must place on record the fact that the resource and administrative implications will have to be taken into account by the government when they introduce the commencement orders for these measures' (91 H of C Official Report 522, 11 April 1986).

106   A Framework for Local Community Care Charters in England, Department of Health, October 1994.

Duties and Powers

Health

. . . .

Introduction

302. The Secretary of State for Health, Health Authorities and NHS Trusts also have statutory duties and responsibilities towards students with learning difficulties and/disabilities. Certain duties are also specific to the Secretary of State for Health and these too are discussed below (see paragraphs 307 to 309).

Duties and powers of health authorities

303. The duties of health authorities (HAs) towards students with learning difficulties and/or disabilities are largely set out in the National Health Service Act 1977 (the 1977 Act).[107] For the most part the services to be provided by HAs to such students will fall under their general duties (delegated to them by the Secretary of State for Health under the provisions of the Act) to provide services to promote the physical and mental health of the population of their respective areas as a whole. Few specific duties are given that are of relevance to the subject of this report, although sections 5(1) and (1A) of the 1977 Act do create a duty to provide for medical and dental inspections, treatment and education of pupils at schools.

304. HAs are also one of those agencies which have a duty[108] to have regard to the Code of Practice on the Identification and Assessment of Special Educational Needs. HAs are required to have extensive involvement in the identification and assessment of special educational needs by the Code, particularly in the provision of medical advice to LEAs and in the appointment of a designated medical officer to co-ordinate health service input into assessment proceedings. HAs are also legally required to be involved in the assessment and statementing process by

virtue of The Education (Special Educational Needs) Regulations 1994.

305. Other duties placed on HAs[109] are found in:

- the Disabled Persons (Services, Consultation and Representation) Act 1986, and specifically section 7[110] which places duties on HAs in respect of persons discharged from hospital (including after detention under the Mental Health Act 1983);

- the Mental Health Act 1983. Section 117 of this Act requires HAs to provide after-care services for a person who has been detained in hospital under the Mental Health Act 1983 where that person is likely to be resident in the district of the health authority when he is released or will be sent to that district;

- the Education Act 1993. Section 166 of this Act requires an HA to help an LEA in the exercise of any of its functions by taking any action specified by the LEA. The HA must comply with the request unless it considers that the help asked for is not necessary, or that having regard to the resources available to them it is not reasonable for them to comply with the request.

NHS trusts

306. NHS trusts do not have any express duties to young persons with learning difficulties and/or disabilities. However, as the 'providers' of care in the NHS internal market, HAs and GP fundholders may purchase health services from trusts for their benefit. Arguably for this reason trusts also have a duty to have regard to the Code, but as they have no direct responsibilities under it, this duty is largely academic.

Secretary of State

307. As stated above, most of the Secretary of State's duties under the 1977 Act are delegated to health authorities to exercise on a day-to-day basis. However there is one specific power that has been retained centrally which is of relevance and this is the Secretary of State's power under section 5(2)(a) to provide 'invalid carriages'[111] for persons who appear to be suffering from a 'severe physical defect or disability' or another vehicle if the disabled person expresses a preference for this. The powers of the Secretary of State also extend to providing or making a grant towards the provision of an adapted vehicle for use of the disabled person in question, providing maintenance and repair services, paying for the insurance and excise duty on any vehicle and building garages to keep it in. Grants may also be made for fuel and driving instruction.

308. The Secretary of State's section 5(2)(a) powers in respect of providing specially adapted vehicles and wheelchairs are now operated through the Motability scheme. Motability is a charitable company (ie, it is non-profit making and non-political) that operates, amongst other things, the government's Mobility Equipment Fund. In general, the scheme allows persons who receive Disability Living Allowance to lease or purchase specially adapted new and used cars and wheelchairs.[112]

309. Entitlement under the Motability scheme is largely determined by entitlement to Disability Living Allowance and Severe Disablement Allowance.[113] For the purpose of the latter a person must be at least 80% disabled to be able to claim.

ENDNOTES

107 A number of duties and powers set out in the NHS Act 1977 are expressed to belong to the Secretary of State for Health. In fact the majority of these are delegated to health authorities pursuant to the National Health Service Functions (Directions to Authorities and Administration Arrangements) Regulations 1996 (SI No. 708).

108 Section 157(2) Education Act 1993.

109 See paragraph 353 on the establishment of 'District Handicap Teams' and DHSS Circular HC(78)5.

110 Compare the duty placed on local authorities by the same section.

111 These are defined by paragraph 4 of Schedule 2 of the 1977 Act as a mechanically propelled vehicle specially designed and constructed (and not merely adapted) for the use of a person suffering some physical defect or disability and used solely by such person.

112 To qualify for the scheme the disabled person need not necessarily be the intended driver of the car. The most severely disabled persons may be awarded grants from the Mobility Equipment Fund.

113 For entitlement to these benefits and an explanation of '80% disabled' see paragraph 334.

Employment

● ●

Introduction[114]

310. The first move towards a legal regime designed to assist disabled persons to find and keep employment was made during the 1939–45 war in the form of the Disabled Persons (Employment) Act 1944. The prime purpose of the Act was to encourage employers to take on more disabled persons by the setting of quotas. These provisions have now been prospectively repealed, and are expected to cease to apply from the end of 1996.

Duties and powers of the Secretary of State

311. However, the 1944 Act will still impose certain duties on and give certain powers to the Secretary of State[115] particularly:

- a power to provide (or to give grants to local authorities for this purpose)[116] certain facilities for disabled persons and who by reason of the nature or severity of their disablement are unlikely either at any time or until after the lapse of a prolonged period to be able otherwise to find employment or to undertake work on their own account. These powers have been used to set up 'Supported Employment' schemes under which severely disabled persons can obtain employment in supported placements, Remploy factories and workshops run by local authorities and voluntary organisations, and through the Remploy Interwork placements scheme;[117]

- a duty to establish a National Advisory Council to advise and assist the Secretary of State generally on matters relating to the employment of disabled persons generally and District Advisory Councils[118] to advise on matters relating to employment and training on a local basis.

312. Another significant piece of legislation dealing with the employment of disabled persons is the Employment and Training Act 1973 (the 1973 Act). This creates a power for the Secretary of State to make arrangements to assist people to select, train for, obtain and retain employment suitable for their ages and capacities and also to assist employers to obtain suitable employees. The 1973 Act also creates a specific power for the Secretary of State to make arrangements for encouraging increases in the opportunities that are available to 'disabled persons'.[119] Various scheme have been operated under this power for a number of years. The latest scheme to be set up under this power is the Access to Work programme which commenced in June 1994. This programme offers practical help and guidance to both employers and disabled persons including paying for:

- a communicator for people who are deaf or hearing impaired;

- a part-time reader or assistance at work for blind people;

- support workers;

- equipment or adaptations to existing equipment to suit disabled persons' needs;

- adaptations for cars, or taxi fares if a person cannot use public transport to get to work;

- alterations to premises or the working environment.

Careers services

313. The 1973 Act[120] also places a duty on the Secretary of State to ensure the provision of careers services to assist young persons who are in or within two years of leaving full-time or part-time vocational education

●   **77** (other than higher education). The duty is owed to all young people and not just students who have learning difficulties and/or disabilities, but it is of equal if not greater importance to this latter group.[121]

The Secretary of State is given a specific duty under the Trade Union Reform and Employments Rights Act 1993 legislation to 'have regard' to the requirements of disabled persons who remain in the statutory client group until they are settled in their career intention. Broadly, the role of careers services is to help young people:

- determine what career would be suitable for them;

- determine what training they need to follow their chosen career;

- find suitable employment or training.

314. In order to exercise his duties to provide careers services the Secretary of State has rights under the 1973 Act to make arrangements with:

  - LEAs;

  - any other person (this includes a private business providing careers services);

  - LEAs and other persons acting jointly; or

- to give directions to LEAs to arrange for the provision of careers services, including a right to require LEAs to contract out careers services.

315. In doing either of these things the Secretary of State is under a duty under the 1973 Act to 'have regard'[122] to the requirements of disabled persons. In fact most services are provided by private providers under contracts from April 1996.

316. Careers services also have functions under the Code of Practice on the Identification and Assessment of Special Educational Needs towards students with special educational needs. In particular, the Code, and Regulation 16(3) of the Education (Special Educational Needs) Regulations 1994, require careers services to be invited

to attend the first annual review of a child's statement after his fourteenth birthday and all subsequent reviews, and the careers officer with special responsibility for disabled young people is required to provide 'continuing oversight of, and information on, the young person's choice of [further education and/or training] provision'. Careers services are also required to assist LEAs in securing such provision.

The Disability Discrimination Act 1995

317. The Disability Discrimination Act 1995 (the 1995 Act) extends the protection and strengthens the position of a disabled person in the areas of employment, the provision of goods, facilities and services, education, access to transport and to premises.

318. Like earlier anti-discrimination legislation, the 1995 Act works by defining discrimination and then outlawing it in certain defined situations. In looking at the 1995 Act it is essential to understand the definition of 'disabled' as this gives the boundaries within which the 1995 Act operates. Section 1(1) of the Act defines a person as disabled if:

> . . . he has a physical or mental impairment which has a substantial and long-term adverse effect on his ability to carry out normal day-to-day activities.

319. The Act therefore protects any person who has an impairment which has a long-term adverse effect upon their ability to complete normal everyday activities. This has to be 'substantial' and can originate from a cause which is either mental or physical. In section 2 the definition is extended to include a person who has had such a disability in the past.

320. The effects of the impairment need only have lasted or be likely to last 12 months in order for a person to qualify as disabled, and a person can still be disabled if his disability occurs only intermittently or is controlled by drugs or in some other way.

Duties and Powers

321. Schedule 1 to the Act gives detailed guidance on the definition of disability. It is notable that the Secretary of State has wide order-making powers to include or exclude certain conditions from the definition of disability.

322. The principal areas in which discrimination against disabled people is outlawed are the supply of goods, facilities and services, disposal of premises and employment. In the education context it is the supply of goods, facilities and services which is the most important.

Supply of goods, facilities and services

323. If a provider of goods or services (the provider) treats a disabled person less well than he treats a non-disabled person, then he is said to 'discriminate' against him for the purposes of the 1995 Act.

324. A number of fairly limited circumstances are also set out as 'justifying' such discrimination, in which case it will not be illegal.

325. A provider who has a practice or policy which makes it impossible or unreasonably difficult for disabled persons to make use of his goods, facilities or services is also required to take all reasonable steps to ensure that a disabled person can make use of them. If the nature or construction of a building prevents a disabled person from using the premises, or makes it unreasonably difficult, the offending features may have to be removed or adapted.

326. However, this does not apply wholesale to the provision of education. The sections which outlaw discrimination in the provision of goods and services do not apply to education which is funded by a 'relevant' body (which includes an extensive, we are tempted to say, comprehensive range of funding authorities and councils), or which in any event is provided at any establishment funded by such a body or any other establishment defined as a school. This

seems to exclude most of the actual provision of 'education' in the narrow sense. This does not extend so far as to exclude the provision of other related services, such as a canteen or a student bar, accommodation, laundry facilities and any other services that can be seen to be separate from the actual process of educating.

327. Thus an educational establishment can discriminate in offering the service of education to disabled people, but cannot discriminate in offering any services ancillary to the education provided.

328. In addition the providers of education will be required under section 29 to include within their annual reports information regarding arrangements for the admission of disabled pupils, steps to avoid disabled students from being treated less favourably than other students and facilities to assist the disabled student in gaining access to their school or college. Under section 30 colleges will be required to publish periodic statements containing relevant information.

Employment

329. The 1995 Act also covers employment, placing an employer in the same, or a very similar position in respect of discrimination against a disabled person as in the parallel fields of sex and race discrimination.

330. An employer discriminates against a disabled person if, for a reason which relates to the disabled person's disability, he treats him less favourably than he treats or would treat others to whom that reason does not or would not apply, and he cannot show that the treatment in question is justified.

331. Unlike the pre-existant anti-discrimination laws, there is no distinction made between 'indirect' and 'direct' discrimination under the 1995 Act. (Indirect discrimination occurs where an employer imposes a condition upon all employees which in practice cannot be met by as many members of the disadvantaged group as

members of the favoured group.) The 1995 Act requires that a disabled person must not be treated less favourably for a reason which relates to his disability. This is thought to be sufficiently broad as a concept so as to cover most indirect discrimination against disabled people.

332. In addition, an employer is under a duty to take reasonable steps to prevent any physical feature of his premises or certain arrangements made by him, from placing a disabled employee at a substantial disadvantage in comparison with those who are not disabled.

Duties and Powers

ENDNOTES

114 This section has been substantially rewritten since the presentation of Part I of this report to reflect the enactment of the Disability Discrimination Act 1995.

115 The Secretary of State is required to have regard to the desirability of appointing persons with experience of working with young disabled persons when appointing any advisers to advise him with respect to the carrying out of his duties under the 1973 Act.

116 Local authorities derive their powers for making arrangements with the Secretary of State for Employment to provide 'sheltered employment' for disabled persons under section 3 of the Disabled Persons (Employment) Act 1958.

117 Remploy is a nationwide organisation operating a placement scheme similar to the Supported Placement Scheme with employers called Remploy Interwork.

118 District Advisory Councils – now known as Committees for the Employment of People with Disabilities – can be contacted through any local Jobcentre or Department of Employment Office.

119 Section 2(2).

120 Sections 8-10. These sections are inserted by the Trade Union Reform and Employment Rights Act 1993 ('TURER'). Formerly the duty fell on local education authorities.

121 The Secretary of State also has a power under the 1973 Act to provide careers services for those not in full-time or part-time education.

122 See comments on the meaning of a duty to 'have regard' to something in paragraphs 101 and 102.

Social Security

● ●

Duties and powers

333. When speaking of social security, it is probably more meaningful to talk of students' entitlement than of the powers and duties of the Benefits Agency. The entitlements to receive assistance and the specific benefits that would be available to students in the 16-plus age range who are 'disabled' are as follows:[123]

(1) Subject to the provisions of this Act, a person shall be entitled to the care component of a disability living allowance for any period throughout which –

(a) he is so severely disabled physically or mentally that –

   (i) he requires in connection with his bodily functions attention from another person for a significant portion of the day (whether during a single period or a number of periods); or

   (ii) he cannot prepare a cooked main meal for himself if he has the ingredients; or

(b) he is so severely disabled physically or mental that, by day, he requires from another person –

   (i) frequent attention throughout the day in connection with his bodily functions; or

   (ii) continual supervision throughout the day in order to avoid substantial danger to himself or others; or

(c) he is so severely disabled physically or mentally that, at night –

   (i) he requires from another person prolonged or repeated attention in connection with his bodily functions; or

   (ii) in order to avoid substantial danger to himself or others he requires another person to be awake for a prolonged period or at frequent intervals for the purpose of watching over him.

Section 72, Social Security Contributions and Benefits Act 1992

A disabled students' benefits pack setting out entitlement to benefits is available free of charge from the Benefits Agency[124].

Definitions of 'disability' in social security legislation

334. The relevant definitions of disablement under the social security legislation depend on what benefit is being claimed. Under provisions in the Social Security Contributions and Benefits Act 1992,[125] Severe Disablement Allowance (SDA) may be payable to a person who has been continuously incapable for work for at least 28 weeks starting on or before their twentieth birthday. These people may qualify on incapacity alone. People who first become incapable of work after their twentieth birthday may qualify if they are incapable of work and disabled and have been so for at least 28 weeks. A person is disabled for SDA purposes if he or she 'suffers from loss of physical or mental faculty such that the extent of the resulting disablement amounts to not less than 80%'. This figure is taken from prescribed degrees of disablement for particular injuries set out in the Social Security (General Benefits) Regulations 1982, Schedule 2. So, for example, Schedule 2 classifies a person who is absolutely deaf as being 100% disabled whereas loss of a thumb is assessed at 30%.

335. A disabled student may also claim Disability Living Allowance which entails:

- a care component; and
- a mobility component.

The disability criteria for eligibility for the care component are set out in Section 72 of the 1992 Act and the Secretary of State has powers to prescribe what circumstances meet the conditions of these sections but to a great extent the provisions speak for themselves as to what 'level' of disability grants entitlement.

336. Eligibility for the mobility component is set out in section 73 if the 1992 Act and arises where:

- a person has a physical disability which renders him unable to walk or virtually unable to do so; or

- he is both blind **and** deaf **and** satisfies any other conditions the Secretary of State may prescribe; or

- he is severely mentally impaired and displays severe behavioural problems and satisfies both of the conditions for the care component set out in sections 72(1)(b) and (c) of the Act;[126] or

- he is able to walk but is so severely disabled physically or mentally that, disregarding any ability he may have to use routes which are familiar to him on his own, he can take advantage of the facility out of doors without guidance or supervision from another person most of the time.

The Secretary of State has a duty to make regulations to define the cases of disablement constituting severe mental impairment and severe behavioural problems. The Secretary of State also has a power to prescribe what is meant by other conditions for entitlement.

337. Another significant benefit due specifically to disabled persons is the Disability Working Allowance. Entitlement to this benefit will arise if at the time of the claim, a person is:

- engaged or normally engaged in remunerative work for at least 16 hours a week; and

- he has a physical or mental disability which puts him at a disadvantage in getting a job; and

- his income and capital falls within prescribed limits.

The Secretary of State once again has powers to prescribe the circumstances which constitute physical or mental disability.

338. It is not intended to repeat the detailed provisions of social security regulations in this report and in any event these would prove of little use in defining appropriate definitions of disability in the fields of health, welfare or education. It is submitted that the relatively rigid and formulaic entitlements set out in regulations determining financial entitlement (and designed to prevent disputes and minimise the role of the courts) are not in tune with the more impressionistic and inclusive approach towards disablement of the other legislation discussed in this report. This latter approach would appear far more appropriate in providing for the health, welfare and educational needs of young people.

Incapacity benefit

339. Certain students, who have paid sufficient qualifying national insurance contributions, may also qualify for the new benefit known as 'incapacity benefit' which replaces invalidity and sickness benefits. Incapacity benefit is designed to provide assistance for those who cannot work due to illness or disability and who are not entitled to statutory sick pay. Incapacity is assessed by an adjudication officer. Where the applicant has a usual occupation then for the first 28 weeks of a claim the applicant will be assessed to see whether he or she is capable of carrying out their normal job. This is the 'own work' test. After 28 weeks (or straightaway in the case of someone who does not have an habitual occupation) an assessment is carried out to see whether a claimant is capable of work in general rather than just simply his usual employment ('the all work test'). Failure to pass this test will result in incapacity benefit ceasing to be paid. Certain disabled persons are exempted from the 'all work' test including those with 'severe learning disability', the paralysed and the registered blind. This list of exemptions is extensive and should cover most forms of disablement although only the more severe forms of learning difficulty will give rise to exemption from the test. Table 3 sets out the relevant legislation and benefit entitlements.

Duties and Powers

Table 3

Regulations (as amended)	Benefits	Eligibility	Financial assistance
Income Support (General) Regulations SI 1987/1967	Income Support	18+ and not in full-time education; or Student if blind, deaf, disabled	Means tested; Not dependent on NI contributions; Higher rates for disabled people
Income Support (General) Regulations SI 1987/1967	Income Support Premiums	Disabled and: – on DLA, IB or SLA; – have invalid carriage; or – registered blind	
Social Security (Severe Disablement Allowance) Regulations SI 1984/1303	Severe Disablement Allowance (SDA)	Students under 19 if studying less than 21 hours per week (ie; teaching and supervised study is less than 21 hours)	Not dependent on NI contributions; Tax free
Social Security (Disability Living Allowance) Regulations SI 1991/2890	Disability Living Allowance (DLA)	Under 65 and need help with personal care or has mobility needs due to disability 3-month period	Not dependent on NI contributions; Tax free
Disability Working Allowance (General) Regulations SI 1991/2887	Disability Working Allowance (DWA)	Over 16, working 16+ hours per week Entitled to DLA, IB or SLA	Means tested; Not dependent on NI contributions
Social Security (Invalid Care Allowance) Regulations SI 1976/409	Invalid Care Allowance	Carer for 35+ hours per week of severely disabled person receiving DLA, IB or SLA at middle or higher rate	Taxable
Various Regulations made under the National Health Service Act 1977	NHS Costs: – dental* – prescriptions/drugs* – optical treatment* – travel costs	* Benefits available to people under 19 and in full-time education On Income Support	100%
Housing Benefit (General) Regulations 1987/1971	Housing Benefit	Under 19 and on course of further education	Means tested
Child Benefit (General) Regulations SI 1976/965	Child Benefit	Under 19 and on course of non-advanced education (full-time)	
Social Security (Incapacity for Work) (General) Regulations	SI 1995/311 Incapacity Benefit ('IB')	Under minimum pension age and incapable of work	Dependent on NI contributions Taxable
Section 5(2)(a) NHS Act 1977	Motability Scheme	Entitled to DLA, IB or SLA	

ENDNOTES

123 Only benefits that are specifically due on account of disability are discussed.

124 An executive agency of the Department for Social Security.

125 Section 68(6).

126 See extracted sections following paragraph 333.

Collaboration Between Agencies

Introduction

340. The draftsmen of the legislation and related codes of practice covering the area of learning difficulties and disabilities clearly foresaw the need for inter-agency co-operation to secure the best results for students and in particular young people aged 18 and under. This trend has gathered pace in more recent legislation and in many cases, for example in the Code of Practice on the Identification and Assessment of Special Educational Needs, detailed mechanisms are put into place to ensure that high-quality interaction between agencies is an everyday feature of the operation of legislation.

341. To the extent not already discussed in previous sections of this report, the statutory requirements for co-operation under some of the major pieces of legislation are set out below together with a discussion of how the interaction of various agencies might in practice be extended. It should be noted that it is difficult from a purely legal point of view to comment on where there are gaps in how agencies work together on the ground. This is a matter for those involved in working with students with learning difficulties and/or disabilities on a day-to-day basis. However, obvious opportunities for greater co-operation that appear to have been missed by the legislation and guidance to date are pointed out wherever possible.

The National Health Service Act 1977

342. The NHS Act 1977 is a relatively early example of agencies having a duty placed upon them to co-operate with other public bodies operating in the same field. In particular, the Act formally requires local authorities[127] and health authorities to co-operate with one another 'in order to secure and advance the health and welfare of the people of England and Wales'.

343. The form such co-operation takes is in the establishment of joint consultative committees (JCCs),[128] whose role is to advise bodies[129] represented on them:

- on the planning and operation of their duties under the 1977 Act; and

- on the planning and operation of services of common concern to those authorities.

344. The JCC model is an interesting one, and the question naturally arises whether there is scope for using this model to any effect in the context of agencies with duties towards students with learning difficulties and/or disabilities. However, to the extent that such committees would merely formalise arrangements already put into practice, for example, by the Code of Practice, this may be unnecessary. The worth of such committees may lie in promoting the interests of maturer students with learning difficulties and/or disabilities, who receive relatively little protection under the various legislation affecting them and who fall outside the DfEE Code. However, it is doubtful whether formal committees on this model would be needed if a Code of Practice for further education were introduced.

The Children Act 1989 and other welfare legislation

345. This legislation contains detailed provision for co-operation between all the various agencies, voluntary organisations and other bodies and individuals who have

or may have a role to play in the life of a child 'in need'.

346. The main provision in the 1989 Act which is expressly designed to secure co-operation between agencies is found in section 27 and comprises a broad general duty placed on all agencies listed in the section[130] to comply with a request from a local authority for their help in exercise of their various functions under Part III of the Children Act 1989 (Local Authority Support for Children and Families). The agency who is in receipt of such a request by the local authority to carry out any specified action is not bound to comply where it is incompatible with its statutory or other[131] duties and does not unduly prejudice the discharge of any of its functions. There is an express duty in section 27(4) placed on local authorities to assist LEAs with the provision of services for any child within the local authority's area who has special educational needs.

> (1) Where it appears to a local authority that any authority . . . mentioned in subsection (3) could, by taking any specified action, help in the exercise of any of their functions under this Part, they may request the help of that other authority . . . specifying the action in question.
>
> (2) An authority whose help is so requested shall comply with the request if it is compatible with their own statutory or other duties and obligations and does not unduly prejudice the discharge of any of their functions.
>
> (3) The [authorities] are:
> (a) any local authority;
> (b) any local education authority;
> (c) any local housing authority;
> (d) any health authority [or National Health Service Trust]; and
> (e) any person authorised by the Secretary of State for the purposes of this section.
>
> (4) Every local authority shall assist any local education authority with the provision of services for any child within the local authority's area who has special educational needs.
>
> *Section 27 – Children Act 1989*

347. Analogously section 47 of the 1989 Act places a duty on named authorities[132] to assist the local authority in any enquiries which they are undertaking to enable the authority to decide whether they should be taking any steps to safeguard or protect a child's welfare.

> (1) Where a local authority:
> (a) are informed that a child who lives, or is found, in their area:
> > (i) is the subject of an emergency protection order; or
> > (ii) is in police protection; or
> (b) have reasonable cause to suspect that a child who lives, or if found, in their area is suffering, or is likely to suffer, significant harm;
>
> the authority shall make, or cause to be made, such enquiries as they consider necessary to enable them to decide whether they should take any action to safeguard or promote the child's welfare.
>
> . . . (9) Where a local authority are conducting enquiries under this section, it shall be the duty of any person mentioned in subsection (11) to assist them with those enquiries (in particular by providing relevant information and advice) if called upon by the authority to do so.
>
> (10) Subsection (9) does not oblige any person to assist a local authority where doing so would be unreasonable in all the circumstances of the case.
>
> The persons are –
> (a) any local authority
> (b) any local education authority
> (c) any housing authority
> (d) any health authority or National Health Service Trust; and
> (e) any person authorised by the Secretary of State for the purposes of this section.
>
> *Section 47 – Children Act 1989*

Duties and Powers

348. The 1989 Act also contains extensive provisions relating to the need for consultation and information flows between agencies particularly in respect of children coming in and out of local authority care. This collaborative approach is emphasised to an even greater extent by the relevant Children Act circulars published by the Department of Health and particularly in regard to the period of transition from full-time school or further education to the outside world.

The Education Act 1993 and the Code of Practice on the Identification and Assessment of Special Educational Needs

349. The Education Act 1993 (the 1993 Act) and particularly the accompanying Code of Practice contain some of the most comprehensive requirements to be found in any of the relevant legislation or guidance. As discussed throughout this report, both the 1993 Act and the Code envisage an interactive approach towards children with special educational needs involving parents, LEAs, schools, social services departments, health authorities and GPs.

350. Statutory expression of the requirement to co-operate is found in section 166 of the 1993 Act. Tracking the wording of similar provisions in the Children Act 1989, the section gives powers to LEAs to call upon local authorities and district health authorities to take specified actions where it appears to the LEA in question that such actions would help in the exercise of their duties in respect of children with special educational needs. Health authorities (HAs) and local authorities are only allowed to decline to take such action on certain specified grounds. These include, for HAs at least, if they believe that having regard to the resources available to them under the 1977 Act it is not reasonable[133] for them to comply with such a request.

(1)   Where it appears to a local education authority that any District Health Authority or local authority could, by taking any specified action, help in the exercise of any of their functions . . . they may request the help of the authority, specifying the action in question.

(2)   An authority whose help is so requested shall comply with the request unless:

(a)   they consider that the help is not necessary for the purpose of the exercise by the local education authority of those functions; or

(b)   subsection (3) below applies.

(3)   This subsection applies:

(a)   in the case of a District Health Authority, if that authority consider that, having regard to the resources available to hem for the purpose of the exercise of their functions under the National Health Service Act 1977, it is not reasonable for them to comply with the request; or

(b)   in the case of a local authority, if that authority considers that the request is not incompatible with their own statutory or other duties and obligations or unduly prejudices the discharge of any of their functions.

(4)   Regulations may provide that, where an authority is under a duty by virtue of subsection (2) above to comply with a request to help a local education authority in the making of an assessment under section 167 of this Act or a statement under section 168 of this Act, they must, subject to prescribed exceptions, comply with the request within the prescribed period.

Section 166(1)-(4) – Education Act 1993

351. There are also requirements under the 1993 Act for LEAs and schools' governing bodies, when reviewing their special educational needs policies and arrangements, to consult with other parties to the extent that it appears necessary or desirable for the purpose of co-ordinating their provision for children with special educational needs. It is left to the discretion

Duties and Powers

of LEAs and schools as to when such consultation is desirable. However, the guidance[134] does state that the Funding Agency for Schools should be consulted and gives examples of where consultation would be appropriate.

352. A more detailed and extensive framework for co-operation and interaction between agencies is given in the Code of Practice and in The Education (Special Educational Needs) Regulations 1994 (SI 1047). Examples of where co-operation is stipulated or encouraged by the Code include:

- paragraph 2:40: representatives from LEAs, health services and social services departments (SDDs) are encouraged to meet together on a 'reasonably regular basis' to plan and co-ordinate activity. The Code acknowledges that what will happen on the ground will vary according to local circumstances;

- paragraph 2:54: social services departments are required to designate an officer or officers responsible for working with schools and LEAs on behalf of children with special educational needs and to whom schools and LEAs should refer for advice. SSDs should ensure that all schools in their area know the name of, and how to contact, a designated social services officer who has responsibilities for special educational needs;

- paragraphs 3:116 and 3:117: LEAs are required to copy notice of their proposal to make a statutory assessment to the social services department[135] and to seek advice as to whether the SSD is aware of any particular problems affecting the child or can provide relevant advice. LEAs and SSDs are encouraged to agree the procedures that will apply when LEAs notify their intention to make assessments and it is suggested that social services departments may wish to combine any assessments to be made

under the Children Act 1989 with special educational needs assessments under the Education Acts 1993;

- paragraphs 4:32 and 4:34: particular attention is paid to the need of the health services and LEAs to co-operate over any non-educational provision to be specified in a child's statement. For example speech therapy may be non-educational or educational provision depending on the child's history and development, although prime responsibility for providing speech therapy now rests with the NHS;[136]

- paragraphs 6:43 to 6:45: a detailed regime requiring co-operation between LEAs and the various agencies who may be expected to play a major role during the post-school years is set out in the Code to cover annual reviews of a child's statement after his fourteenth birthday up to the age of 19. LEAs are required to invite SSDs to each review meeting to ensure that any parallel assessment being made under the NHS and Community Care Act 1990, the Chronically Sick and Disabled Persons Act and the Disabled Persons (Services, Consultation and Representation) Act 1986 can contribute to and draw information from the review process. In each annual review after the age of 14 a 'Transition Plan' must be drawn up or amended to 'plan coherently for the young person's transition to adult life' and LEAs are encouraged to consider sending a copy of the transition plan and the review report to the FEFC, particularly where specialist college provision outside the FE sector may be required.

The joint circular on assessments and statements of special educational needs

353. The requirement for inter-agency cooperation is also reflected in circulars on the issue. In particular Joint Circular HN(89)20/HN(FP)(19)/LASSL(89)7/WOC54/89 /DES:22/89 on Assessments and Statements

of Special Educational Needs: Procedures within the Education, Health and Social Services clearly accepts that assessment of children with special educational needs cannot be viewed as a single agency approach. Setting out requirements for an inter-disciplinary approach, which have since been repeated and augmented and now set out comprehensively in the Code of Practice, the Circular also stresses the importance, in the case of severely handicapped children in particular, of the use of District Handicap Teams:

> *The complexity of the needs of some individual children may call for the involvement of additional professional help including the family doctor. Authorities are reminded of the advice given in DHSS Circular HC(78)5 that District Handicap Teams (DHTs) (or District Child Development Teams where they exist) should strengthen the multi-disciplinary approach to the needs of severely disabled children including the under-fives. Where they exist DHTs may offer a suitable vehicle for the assessment of these children's special educational needs. Community Mental Handicap teams may have a role to play. The child, adolescent and family psychiatric services, whether hospital or community based, may be an appropriate source of advice about children with emotional or behavioural problems.*

ENDNOTES

127 Local authorities exercise 'Care in the Community' functions (home help and laundry) under sections 21 and Schedule 8 of the 1977 Act.

128 Pursuant to section 22(2) of the NHS Act 1977. The proceedings and membership of the committee is governed by the Joint Consultative Order 1985 and their proceedings are required to be made public by virtue of the Health Service Joint Consultative Committees (Access to Information) Act 1986.

129 In addition to any local, health authorities or family practitioner committees represented by JCCs, the Joint Consultative Committees Order 1985 provides that three representatives of voluntary organisations who appear to have an interest in services of common concern should be appointed to each JCC.

130 The Secretary of State has powers to expand the application of the section by 'authorising' persons under section 27(3). The Secretary of State 'authorised' FE colleges in this manner in 1994. Analogous powers exist in relation to section 47 (see paragraph 347 below) and FE colleges have also been authorised under this section.

131 The reference to other duties is not defined. It is presumably meant to refer to contractual obligations and such other common law duties such as the duty to exercise reasonable care and not to perform negligent acts or omissions.

132 The FEFC was 'authorised' as a person to whom section 47(9) applies in 1994.

133 The judicial interpretation of 'reasonableness' is an objective standard.

134 DES Circular 6/94.

135 Regulation 5 of The Education (Special Education Needs) Regulations 1994 SI No:1047.

136 Who is to pay for speech therapy has in the past been a bone of contention as part of more general debate as to what is educational and what is non-educational provision. In R v Lancashire County Council, ex parte M [1989] 2 FLR 279 (Court of Appeal) the court rejected claims that speech therapy could not be special educational provision (and thus not the financial responsibility of LEAs) and stated that there was a duty on LEAs to provide special educational provision even though the employees to provide it were not in their direct employment. The Education (Special Educational Needs) Regulations 1994 and the Code of Practice, requires LEAs to specify in Part 6 of a statement the non-educational provision which is required to meet the child's SEN and which the LEA propose to make available or are satisfied will be purchased by the DHA, GP fundholder or others. The designated medical officer is required to liaise as is necessary to ensure that the Health Service contribution is confirmed. By means of this liaison mechanism decisions as to who should pay for any type of provision should have been made before the statement is finalised. However, paragraph 4:35 of the Code of Practice makes clear that where a child's statement specifies speech therapy as an educational provision and the NHS have not agreed to provide the speech therapy in question, then the ultimate responsibility for ensuring that the provision is made rests with the LEA unless the child's parents have made appropriate arrangements. As to the dividing line between educational and non-educational provision, in many cases the distinction would presumably be obvious. However, in grey areas such as speech therapy the problem of allocating responsibility will remain. The Code makes clear that the NHS is expected to take prime responsibility for this area although in each individual case whether provision is educational or not will depend on the child's

health and development. In <u>R v Lancashire County Council, ex parte M</u> the court distinguished between speech therapy that was required on purely medical grounds, eg, after an operation, and therapy that is required to correct some chromosomal disorder or social cause which hinders a child's educational development.

Printed in the United Kingdom for The Stationery Office
Dd. 303094C29 10/96